Richard A. Lester
Industrial Relations Section
Princeton University

By FRANK TANNENBAUM

SLAVE AND CITIZEN: *The Negro in the Americas* (1947)

MEXICO: *The Struggle for Peace and Bread* (1950)

A PHILOSOPHY OF LABOR (1951)

These are Borzoi Books, published by

ALFRED A. KNOPF *in New York*

A PHILOSOPHY OF LABOR

A Philosophy OF LABOR

FRANK TANNENBAUM

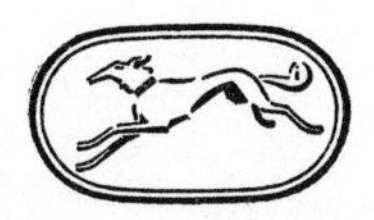

New York : ALFRED · A · KNOPF : *1951*

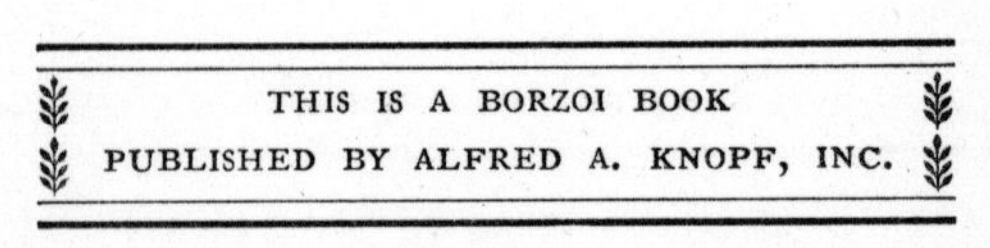

FIRST EDITION

In Memoriam

to

ROBERT BEACH WARREN

ACKNOWLEDGMENTS

THE IDEAS that have gone into the making of this book were first put together in an essay in the spring of 1947, while I was in residence at the Institute for Advanced Study, in Princeton, New Jersey. I owe much to the comment and criticism of Walter Stewart, the late Robert B. Warren, and Winfield Riefler.

John Herman Randall, Jr., read the entire manuscript, and Austin P. Evans the first four chapters. I acknowledge my gratitude to both.

I am indebted to Fon W. Boardman, Jr., for his careful literary criticism.

I also wish to record my indebtedness to my wife, Jane Belo, for her essay on the Balinese temper, from which I learned a great deal.

Much of what I have written in recent years is in some measure due to the receptive and stimulating attitude of John Krout as editor of the *Political Science Quarterly*.

Finally, I want to express my gratitude to Alfred A. Knopf and Harold Strauss for their interest in this volume.

CONTENTS

A PHILOSOPHY OF LABOR

CHAPTER I

The Drift of Our Time

TRADE-UNIONISM is the conservative movement of our time. It is the counterrevolution. Unwittingly, it has turned its back upon most of the political and economic ideas that have nourished western Europe and the United States during the last two centuries. In practice, though not in words, it denies the heritage that stems from the French Revolution and from English liberalism. It is also a complete repudiation of Marxism. This profound challenge to our time has gone largely unnoticed because the trade-union's preoccupation with the detailed frictions that flow from the worker's relation to his job seemed to involve no broad program. In tinkering with the little things—hours, wages, shop conditions, and security in the job—the trade-union is, however, rebuilding our industrial society upon a different basis from that envisioned by the philosophers, economists, and social revolutionaries of the eighteenth and nineteenth centuries.

The importance of trade-unionism has been obscured

until recently by the claims upon public attention of movements of lesser historical significance. The Communist, Fascist, and Nazi eruptions are secondary outcroppings of the same social rift that has brought trade-unionism into being. These popular upheavals are of passing import because they rest upon formal ideologies, subject to modification as the fashions in ideas change. Their dependence upon dogma reveals their inner debility, and their weakness is attested by their readiness to use force to impose upon society the design their ideology calls for. This assumes an ability to model and freeze man within some preconceived mold, which is contrary to experience. The unending flux of the people of the earth cannot be contained in an ideological straitjacket, and those who use violence toward that end are merely digging their own graves, as they always have done.

In contrast with these self-conscious and messianic political movements, the trade-union has involved a clustering of men about their work. This fusion has been going on for a long time. It has been largely unplanned, responsive to immediate needs, irrepressible, and inarticulate of its own ends because, on the whole, it had no general purposes. A sparsity of general ideas and a lack of any "ideology" kept the trade-union movement from being obtrusively vocal and permitted mesmeric political groups to look upon it as something of no great importance. But its very lack of ideas made it strong and enabled it to concentrate upon immediate ends without wasting its energies in a futile pursuit of Utopia. The trade-union movement could go on for generation after generation despite many failures, gradually accommodating itself to a changing industrial environment. It could do that without challenging the political or moral ideas current at the time, all the while slowly shaping new institutions, habits, and loyalties. It has gathered power within the community until it has suddenly dawned upon men that a new force—not an idea, but a new force—has come into being. This force is changing the structure of our economy and redistributing power in our society.

The emphasis in trade-unionism is upon the fusion of men in their respective trades or industries, and upon *movement*. There is nothing static about it, and calling this profound social drift "a problem to be solved" is a quaint commentary upon our optimism. The trade-union movement is not a problem. It is a process giving rise to innumerable conflicts because it has incalculable consequences. Its influence is felt at every point because it affects every aspect of modern society. The trade-union movement—*movement*—is not soluble. There is nothing in modern political wisdom or skill that can write *finis* to this flux, or even give it permanent direction. It is no more a soluble "problem" than the rise of the "middle class" [1] was a "problem" that could have been solved by a feudal society. As we look back upon the centuries of conflict that record the slow and at times violent transition from a feudal to a commercial and industrial com-

[1] I use the term "middle class" in its conventional sense, but I use it reluctantly. It seems to me one of those clichés in the "social sciences," like the word "problem," that we would do better without if we could get rid of it. The whole concept of "class" is a hindrance to social analysis.

monwealth, it is clear that there was nothing the older society could have done to prevent the newer design from taking shape. In time the middle class came to have a special law of its own, and to be organized into a distinct body, the incorporated town with its own charter. It is important for purposes of comparison with the trade-union movement to remember that these changes were not the result of a plan, a philosophy, or even a theory. The rising merchants had no revolutionary objectives. "They only asked of society to make for them a place compatible with the sort of life they were leading." [2]

What the merchants and traders asked from their contemporary feudal institutions was the freedom to come and go as their business required. They wanted their own law, and they urged the "abolition of protestations most incompatible" with their way of life as citizens of a chartered town. Obviously, medieval society was faced with a stubborn "problem," but the real problem was how to meet the newer needs with the least possible violence. So it has been with the trade-union movement. What the workers asked for when the factory had welded them into coherent groups were a few changes in the rules governing their daily labor.

The workers wanted the right: (1) to organize; (2) to bargain collectively; (3) to keep nonmembers off the pay roll; (4) to participate in fixing wages and conditions of labor; (5) to meet freely for their purposes; (6) to define the jurisdiction of their jobs.

[2] Henri Pirenne: *Medieval Cities* (translated from the French by Frank D. Halsey, Princeton University Press, 1925), p. 176.

Like the rising towns that imposed new rules upon medieval society, the trade-unions are forcing basic changes in the laws, practices, and habits that welded modern society into a going concern. The implementation of these union rules has so changed the character of our society as to be comparable to the rise of the bourgeoisie. The growth of the middle class was more significant than the French Revolution, the Reform Bill in Great Britain, the revolutions of 1848 in central Europe, or the hundreds of other political upheavals from the period of the Reformation down to our own time. It is in this sense that the Communist movement in Russia and the Nazi upheaval in Germany are merely incidents in a wider drift of which they are unconscious manifestations.

This wider drift is reflected in the new "society" formed by the workers of the mill, mine, and factory, for whom the trade-union has proved the "natural" instrument, just as the town proved the fitting vehicle for the rising merchants and traders.

The full measure of the trade-union movement can be appreciated only by seeing the role it has played in the lives of the workers in the transition from a simple society to a complex industrial and urban economy. The Industrial Revolution destroyed the solid moorings of an older way of life, and cast the helpless workers adrift in a strange and difficult world. The peasant who had been reared in the intimacy of a small village, where customary values prescribed for every act between the cradle and the grave and where each man played a role in a drama known to all, now found himself isolated and bewildered in a city crowded with strangers and indifferent to a common rule. The symbolic universe that had patterned the ways of men across the ages in village, manor, or guild had disappeared.

This is the great moral tragedy of the industrial system. It destroyed the symbolic and meaningful world that had endowed the life of the individual with an ethical character. The individual worker now had no recognizable place that he could call his own, no society to which he "naturally" belonged, and no values by which he was expected to live. The ordinary meanings that make life acceptable had evaporated. His economic insecurity was but part of a larger perplexity. The rapid growth of factory, town, and city had brought a new world into being.

In 1790 there were in the United States only two large cities, New York and Philadelphia, with about 30,000 people each. Eight of the original thirteen states had no city of more than 8,000 inhabitants, and in all of the nation there were, in addition to New York and Philadelphia, only three other cities that could be considered important—Boston, Baltimore, and Charleston—and these had less than 15,000 dwellers each. Ninety-six per cent of the American people lived in little villages, towns, and the open country.

Today, of course, the picture is almost the reverse. On the evidence of the 1940 census, 92 cities contained over 32,000,000 inhabitants. A hundred and fifty years ago the vast majority of the people in the United States and in the rest of the world lived in rural districts and were self-employed. The cities were small, the markets chiefly parochial; and the families supplied a large part of their own needs by direct and immediate production. Perhaps not more than ten per cent of the people who earned their living by labor were dependent upon a money wage for all of their real income. In the last hundred and fifty years the Industrial Revolution has stripped the mass of men in western Europe and the United States of their self-sufficiency and has driven them from the country and the village to the larger towns and cities. At the same time it has made them dependent on a money wage, not as a supplement to goods they produced themselves, but as the source of all their income. This profound change in the nature of man's relations to his fellows is best characterized by the symbol of the city dweller and the wage worker, including not merely those who work at manual tasks, but all workers in the arts, crafts, and professions as well.

This change is unique for both its rapidity and its inclusiveness. Today in the United States, out of a working population of over 60,000,000, approximately 12,000,000 work for themselves. We have become a nation of employees. We are dependent upon others for our means of livelihood, and most of our people have become completely dependent upon wages. If they lose their jobs they lose every resource, except for the relief supplied by the various forms of social security. Such dependence of the mass of the people upon others for *all* of their income is something new in the world. *For our generation, the substance of life is in another man's hands.*

This dependence upon a job has been a cumulative

process, and has been growing with increasing speed and intensity. In the last two generations the urban drift has become most evident. In 1870, in the United States, 53 per cent of those working for a living were engaged in agriculture. Today only some 13 per cent are working as farmers or farm hands. This unforeseen and unplanned transformation has modified the nature of the society man has always known. The city has disintegrated the extended family that cushioned and protected the individual between the cradle and the grave, served him in his need, and shared with him the pleasures and the sorrows of life. What is left of the family in the urban community is a weak and unstable makeshift for what the race has always known as its most basic and stable institution.

It is against this background that the role of the trade-union must be examined. In terms of the individual, the union returns to the worker his "society." It gives him a fellowship, a part in a drama that he can understand, and life takes on meaning once again because he shares a value system common to others. Institutionally the trade-union movement is an unconscious effort to harness the drift of our time and reorganize it around the cohesive identity that men working together always achieve.

That is why the trade-union is a repudiation of the individualism of the French Revolution and of the liberalism of English utilitarian philosophers. It rests upon the group, upon the organized "society" forged by the mine, mill, and factory. Trade-unionism is a repudiation of Marxism because its ends are moral rather than economic. It is a social and ethical system, not merely an economic one. It is concerned with the whole man. Its ends are the "good life." The values implicit in trade-unionism are those of an older day, antedating the grating modern political slogans. It is an unwitting effort to return to values derived from the past: security, justice, freedom, and faith. It is in those values, explicit and inherent, that man had found his human dignity.

Trade-unionism is counterrevolutionary because it contrives to build these values into our industrial society by working at them specifically and in detail, without any commitment to a general theory or an ideology, and even without a sense of direction. But the sum of these thousands of little acts, precedents, rights, and privileges adds up to a rebuilding of our industrial system along different lines from those on which it first developed and contrary to the designs the social revolutionaries would impose upon it. The trade-union movement is conservative and counterrevolutionary just because it is creative. It builds step by step, and the design expands as a series of new institutions that govern the entire man and increasingly rule the world wherein he has his being. He who would understand the labor movement must look backward and see where it came from. The future direction is to be discerned in the institutional pattern resting on previously established rule, habit, and commitment.

The trade-union's concern with detail is the most important point because it is an attempt to bridge the gap between labor on the one hand and freedom and security on the other. This gap has been one of the prime characteristics of urban industrial society. The union is faced with the question: how can the daily task be made coterminous with the good life, as it always had been until the machine came to make work and life separate things. If man cannot once again make freedom, security, and work synonymous, he will destroy the machine. Our industrial civilization will not survive state planning, Socialist control, Communist bureaucracy, or Fascist moral perversion, for they all postulate this disparity between labor and freedom.

The separation between life and labor, from which so many of our difficulties stem, is implicitly accepted by liberalism and Marxism and explains their failure to develop a satisfying theory for our time. They both assume that the good society can be built upon economic motives. The free competition of the economists and the classless society of the Communists have this in common. They are caught up in the endless beneficence of a money economy. But the bane of our industrial society lies in making income in money coterminous with the ends of life itself. A widening money economy increases the complexity of our society, standardizes the objectives, multiplies the dissatisfactions of all men, drives the society toward equalitarian ends in monetary terms, and universalizes individual insecurity.

If the possession of money is the goal of all our efforts, the lack of it is complete failure, for without it nothing is to be had, not even the barest subsistence. The moral inadequacy of industrialism lies in substituting a "good wage" for the good life.

The trade-union stepped into this breach between the good life and work for a money wage that resulted from the destruction of the earlier cohesive society, and the reduction of man to an isolated individual, hired as a "hand," and paid in cash. Its interests in the detailed relationships between the worker and his employer saved the trade-union from a commitment to any general formula and made it possible for the economists, the liberals, and the Marxists to deny its intrinsic importance. If the economists and liberals considered the trade-union a hindrance to a possible competitive harmony, the Marxists believed that unless they could secure control of the trade-union movement it would prove an impediment in the way of the revolution that would create heaven upon earth by abolishing the source of all evil. The early economists would have put an end to the movement; the Marxists sought to capture it for their own purposes. Neither have had their way. The trade-union movement has survived because it satisfies the human craving for moral status in a recognizable society.

CHAPTER II

The Older Pattern

THE TRADE-UNION movement is an unconscious rebellion against the atomization of industrial society. It suggests that the men, skilled and unskilled, who do the labor of the world want to return to an older and socially "normal" way of life. If the historical record has any meaning, a sense of identity among men laboring at a common task is "natural" and inevitable. Men identified with one another in their daily work develop a sense of their part of the social universe which is peculiarly their own and which they share with no one else. How otherwise explain the world-wide spread of the guild for traders, craftsmen, and artisans? There were guilds in China at least a thousand years ago; in India we know of them in 600 B.C.; they were present in ancient Japan, were widely scattered and of long duration in the Islamic world, were found in Greece, and existed for centuries in Rome and in Europe during the Middle Ages and beyond.

In spite of many differing forms, the guilds satisfied similar needs and were an accepted part of town and city life in many parts of the world. The names by which they were called suggest their role in European society. The term for guild was variously known as: "*Officium* or *ministerium* in Latin, *métier* or *jurande* in French, *arte* in Italian, *ambacht* or *neering* in the Netherlands, *Amt*, *Innung*, *Zunft* or *Handwerk* in German, *craft-gild* or *mistery* in English." [1] These associations lasted through the centuries and were to be found as late as the end of the eighteenth, and in some places persisted into the first part of the nineteenth. The Roman guilds traced their origins back to Numa, the second legendary King of Rome. The goldsmiths, coppersmiths, builders, diggers, shoemakers, doctors, tailors, painters, porters, leather workers, tanners, and others enjoyed a long, though uneven, corporate life. Marcus Aurelius gave them the right to receive legacies and established them as "legal persons." Later emperors, especially Alexander Severus, deliberately formed all trades into guilds. In time they became instruments of governmental control and were used for purposes of tax-collecting.

In some trades no person could escape being a member of a guild. He could not leave it and in later years could be brought back by force as if he were a fugitive. The members were known as "brothers and sisters," and the organizations were self-governing. When the guilds came to be used by the state they had an official *præfect* set over them. These Roman guilds had their special meeting-places and their own clubhouses, and they played an

[1] Henri Pirenne: *Economic and Social History of Medieval Europe* (New York, 1937), pp. 179–80.

important role in the lives of their members.[2] In Roman times, guilds were widespread, and we even know of small towns, such as Oxyrhynchos in Egypt, where the coppersmiths, bakers, beekeepers, and beer- and oil-sellers were all organized.

If the origins of the medieval guilds are obscure, there is general agreement that they were in existence and active late in the eleventh century. We have records showing the presence of weavers' guilds in Mainz in 1099, those of fishmongers at Worms in 1106, of shoemakers at Würzburg in 1128, and of coverlet-weavers at Cologne in 1149. They are even to be found in such little places as Pontoise in 1162, Hagenau in 1164, and Hochfelden and Swindratzheim before 1164. In England the craft guilds are noted in the reign of Henry I (1100-35), in Oxford, Huntingdon, London, Lincoln, and other towns.

These guilds always seemed to carry with them the same sort of group responsibility, special distinction, and social and religious identification that set them apart by themselves. Sometimes the groups were small, as must have been the eleven hundred guilds in Istanbul in 1640. But large or small, these groups had some authority, distinction, and recognizable personality. In England in the reign of Edward III (1327–77) they were so much a part of the life of the municipalities and so important in the regulation of manufactures and trade that a law enacted says that ". . . artificers and men of mysteries

[2] William Stevens Davis: *The Influence of Wealth in Imperial Rome* (New York, 1910), pp. 230–6.

shall each choose his own mystery before the next Candlemas, and having so chosen it he shall henceforth use no other." [3]

Guild membership had thus assumed a legal character, each man belonging to some one craft, and having become a member of one, "he shall henceforth use no other." The guilds' position in the sight of the law varied from time to time and from place to place, but there were long periods during which they had corporate standing, and their decisions were considered as part of the law, or the judges at least took their decisions into consideration. They owned property and had rights upon the property of their members who died intestate. They settled disputes among their members, dealt with questions of hours, wages, quality, apprenticeships, and admissions to the craft and controlled many of the things that are a necessary part of any trade subject to a changing market. Thus in 1418 the barbers in Bristol asked the municipality for the right to elect two "watchers," to be sworn before the mayor. They were to see to it that the barbers' rights were not invaded by members of other trades. The barbers also asked for a seven-year apprenticeship for those who would exercise that trade in the future. These and other rules, they said, were wanted to protect their trade from being destroyed.[4] Membership in some cases became hereditary, so that the descendants of the same family continued in their father's trade.

The political ambitions of the European medieval

[3] Quoted in Stella Kramer: *The English Craft Gilds and the Government* (New York, 1905), p. 37.

[4] Ibid., p. 30.

guilds appeared in some towns as early as the first half of the thirteenth century. They wanted the right to self-government, to meet and talk over their own problems, to have a bell and a seal, and to share in the local government. Opposition to these demands showed itself in Rouen in 1189, in Dinant in 1255, in Brussels in 1290, and in other places. Efforts to prohibit the trade guilds did not stop the movement toward political participation, and we see them getting place and power in many of the towns in western Europe.

In view of the complete organization of all the crafts, they came, in some towns, to be associated with the government. At times they elected a certain number of their own members to the town council, or were allowed to establish a new body of magistrates alongside the older one. Sometimes they secured control of the city treasury by requiring that fiscal matters be submitted for the approval of a delegated body elected by themselves. In certain instances they got control over the town altogether, as they did at Liége, Utrecht, and Cologne. After 1384 the thirty-two craft guilds in Liége dominated the town, and political rights were enjoyed only by those who were inscribed on their roles. They named the council and the governors. The "maîtres" (burgomasters) were recruited by their council, and all important decisions had to be submitted to the thirty-two craft guilds for approval by a majority vote in each one of them.[5]

[5] Henri Pirenne: *Economic and Social History of Medieval Europe*, p. 204.

When we consider the ages spanned, the different cultures, and the contrasting economies, it is surprising how much alike were the objectives sought. The guilds tried to control the labor supply by defining the conditions of entrance into the craft. They regulated wages, hours, prices, quality, and tools to be used. They sought equality for each member; they protected members from undue competition and from injury; and they strove for stability. They kept out "foreigners." They tried to secure complete control over their own parochial market. The monopolistic character of the guilds increased as the towns became more "democratic" and as they achieved greater influence in their own communities. At Ghent, for instance, it was forbidden after 1314 to manufacture cloth within three miles of the city walls, and armed bands destroyed the looms in the surrounding villages if anyone attempted to carry on the outlawed craft.[6]

The histories of non-European guilds reveal similar organizations, methods, and objectives. While we do not have the date of the first Chinese guilds, we know of many Korean guilds with written constitutions that are more than a thousand years old. These make reference to Chinese guilds as original models.[7] Marco Polo speaks of twelve guilds in Hangchow under the reign of Kublai Khan (1260–94), with their separate houses and thousands of members. Of the forty-two Peking guilds studied by Burgess, four date their origin to the Ming dynasty

[6] Ibid., pp. 210–11.

[7] S. D. Gamble and J. S. Burgess: *Peking: A Social Survey* (New York, 1921), p. 166.

(1368–1644).[8] In 1928 there were eleven "professional," forty craft, and sixty commercial guilds in Peking. The list reads like a trade-union directory in any American city. It includes carpenters, furniture-painters, masons, paperhangers, shoemakers, tailors, tinkers, tinsmiths, actors, bakers, cooks, porters, waiters, and a few occupations that are unknown in an American city. There was an active association of the blind, of storytellers, and of wheelbarrow-pushers.

More interesting than their number is their similarity to European guilds. The porters' guild, for instance, limited the area individual members were allowed to work in and imposed a fine upon them if they worked outside their own district. It had an apprentice system and an initiation fee, and apprentices were required to have "guarantors" of good character before admission to the fellowship. In recent years membership was confined to "sons and brothers of guild members." [9] They had their own "elders," who disciplined the members after a public trial and who had the power of expulsion for serious offenses. This organization had its special patron saint and held its yearly meetings at a religious shrine.

The carpenters' guild, like that of the porters, required apprenticeship and an initiation fee before full membership could be secured. In return the member was assured the standard wage and "a proper place for burial." [10] The carpenters had four thousand members

[8] John Stewart Burgess: *The Guilds of Peking* (New York, 1928), p. 77.
[9] Ibid., p. 84.
[10] Ibid., p. 93.

distributed in six groups, and, like other Chinese guilds, held their meetings and festivals in a temple in which the guild's saint was worshipped at a regular yearly religious observance.

The most interesting of the Peking associations was the guild of the blind. Its members made their living by singing and storytelling.

Like similar organizations in other parts of the world, these guilds had rotation in office, a recognized social and religous ceremonial, and regular festivals. They indoctrinated new members into the lore and ethics of the trade and provided for private cemeteries, payment of funeral expenses, and medical help. Some of the guilds fixed prices, and some controlled wages. Many of the guilds had elaborate rules for punishment. Before the days of the Republic they punished grave offenses by applying a bamboo cane to a convicted member. The silk-weavers, on the other hand, imposed the payment for a theatrical performance as a fine for disregarding the rule that weaving must be taught before dyeing.

The importance of the guilds in the Chinese community is reflected in the statement: "It has been the guilds, rather than the government, that have maintained trade standards of weight, measure and quality, though the ones adopted by the different guilds have not necessarily been the same." [11]

In India, as in China, the guilds are an ancient institution. They can be traced back to the sixth century B.C. and are probably older than that. The lawbooks of that

[11] S. D. Gamble and J. S. Burgess, op. cit., p. 191.

period recognize their existence and describe some of their powers. He who disobeys the guild may be banished, and he who fails to perform a contract entered into by the guild may also have his entire property confiscated. The law requires that the king approve whatever guilds do to other people, "whether what they do is cruel or kind."[12] More than that, according to laws that date back some two thousand years, the king was expected to "establish again on the path [of duty] all such as have erred from their own laws, whether family, castes, guilds, associations. . . ."[13]

Some of these guilds were associated in religious fraternities, built temples, and acted as banks, paying a regular interest on funds accepted in trust. All of the occupations were organized, and they were so powerful that non-artisan guilds had to be formed in self-defense.[14] In some towns guilds were coincident with castes. In others there were subdivided guilds in the same caste. More recently some guilds may have a number of different castes. As occupation tends to go by caste, a member of the caste working at a given trade is also a member of the guild. Membership is hereditary in the family, and all sons of a deceased member are automatically admitted into their father's guild without any fees. New members are required to pay an entrance fee.

Guilds tend to become all-powerful, and their practices have a familiar touch to the student of labor in the United States. "Thus in Ahmedabad, as I was told, a banker

[12] E. W. Hopkins: *India, Old and New* (New York, 1902), p. 173.
[13] Ibid., quoted on p. 170.
[14] Ibid., p. 180.

who had half his house tiled got into a quarrel with a confectioner and could not get the other half of his house tiled till the sweetmeat-guild had told the tile-guild that it might resume work for the representative of the bankers' guild." [15]

The Indian guilds, like similar organizations in other parts of the world, tend to fix wages, prices, and working hours and to retain a monopoly over their own craft. And again, as in the Chinese guilds, they tend to retain for internal settlement many disputes that would in other places go to the regular courts. Cases brought into regular courts in some of the large cities are often referred back to the guilds for adjudication. "Every industry or craft was self-governing by its *Sreni* [guild]." [16] The role of the guild was in fulfillment of the Hindu ideal "that economic ends are not ends in themselves, but must subserve to higher religious and spiritual ends of life. Therefore . . . different castes were to pursue different crafts in consonance with the ideals and values for which each caste stood." [17]

These activities, and many others, have been carried on by the Indian guilds for over two thousand years. If the guilds are now declining, they were until recently, and in some of the smaller communities, perhaps, still are, in full possession of their ancient prerogatives.

It is clear not only that for ages before the Industrial Revolution labor was "organized," but also that the guild

[15] Ibid., p. 193.
[16] Radha Kumaud Koukerg: *Ancient Indian Education, Brahmanical and Buddhist* (London, 1947), p. 353.
[17] Ibid., p. 352.

always carried with it a sense of craft, mystery, status, conformity, honor, and responsibility. The "normal" condition of craft organization made it possible and "natural" for every guild to have its particular saint, its niche in the church, its special festivals, its peculiar customs, powers, and laws. These guilds were generally democratically administered, and enforced their decisions by collective actions, boycotts, ostracism, and political influence.

The equivalent of the "society" of the guilds in the towns was provided in the country by the villages. Scholars have differed about the origin of the early villages and have argued the extent of communal landownership. For our purposes, however, it is sufficient to note that the associated design has been as widespread in agriculture as in industry, commerce, and trade. In fact, the presence of some common rules, traditions, and mutually accepted responsibilities can also be found among nomadic tribes. Nowhere has man lived either by himself or for himself. He has always been a member of a group, abided by a common rule, and benefited by the protection thus provided.

Village communities have been described as of three types: the semipermanent, the permanent, and the migratory agricultural village. The last may still be found among the more primitive peoples in the Malay Peninsula and in the Amazon basin. The semipermanent agricultural groups, which may occupy the same site for a number of years, can be seen in southeastern Asia, Melanesia, and large sections of Africa, Borneo, and other places. The permanent agricultural community is spread over Europe, India, China, New Guinea, Mexico, and Central and South America, especially in Ecuador, Peru, and Bolivia.

Among the interesting communal villages is the Zadruga family community among the Serbians. Here is a patriarchal organization, living in a large house, holding its land, livestock, and money in common.[18] This type of organization seems in the past to have extended from the Adriatic into Bulgaria. Similar organization of rural life in the western part of the British Isles until the Middle Ages has been described, as well as among the Irish, and the West Highlanders of Scotland. Here the families lived together, held their land in common for four generations, and divided it up in the fifth. In spite of many differences in size, family structure, forms of landownership, and inheritance, "people appear to have lived in nucleated villages since the dawn of agriculture." [19]

That some sort of associated and organized life should exist in agricultural villages would seem a necessary feature of their survival, but that an organized society should arise and become a widespread institution on the feudal estate is further proof that men, when grouped together physically in their labor, tend to become a community.[20]

[18] Philip Mosely: "The Peasant Family: The Zadruga, or the Communal Joint Family in the Balkans and Its Recent Evaluation," in *The Cultural Approach to History*, edited by Caroline F. Ware (New York: Columbia University Press; 1940), pp. 95–108.

[19] Harold J. E. Peak: "Village Community," *The Encyclopedia of the Social Sciences*, Vol. XV.

[20] The question might arise whether this statement is not so broad

Whatever the origin of the manorial court, it governed the lives of the agricultural plantation in western Europe for hundreds of years, very much the way the guild ruled the industrial scene in the towns and cities during the same period. The feudal system varied from place to place, and the manor, widespread even if not all-pervasive, had distinct forms of seigneurial jurisdiction. "But everywhere it extended at least to all questions concerning holdings, labour services, dues and the cultivation of the soil. Each manor had its court, composed of peasants, presided over by the bailiff or *villicus* and giving judgment according to the 'custom of the manor.' . . ."[21]

The people living on the manor, villeins and freeholders, formed a community bound by custom and abiding by the law declared by the manorial court. The body of the court consisted of its suitors, and was attended by all persons whose tenure, status, or office so required. The court was the common possession of the local community. Judgment was rendered according to the local custom of the manor, and some of these judgments went against the lord.

---

as to bring men living in slavery or confined in prison within this generalization. In fact it does include both slavery and penal institutions. Prisons do become communities. See Frank Tannenbaum: *Crime and the Community* (Boston: Ginn & Co., 1938). Otherwise how explain the repeated prison riots. Very much the same is true of slavery. See Arturo Ramos: *The Negro in Brazil* (Washington, D.C., 1939). For men to act together, they must acquire some sense of identity, common objectives, accepted rules of behavior, and a recognized leadership, and these requirements are met in prison riots as well as in slave rebellions.

[21] Henri Pirenne: *Economic and Social History of Medieval Europe*, p. 63.

In theory, the lord declared the law. In practice, it was pronounced as the ancient custom of the manor by the people, gathered "under the ash tree in the middle court of the abbey," [22] or in the great hall of the castle. Tradition, too, regulated the frequency of the courts' meetings, which might be every three weeks or only twice a year.

The court was the living embodiment of the "customs of the manor," which it declared as the different matters came before it. When changes were made, these found their way into the rolls that contained the record of the proceedings. The lord could make no sudden demands that ran counter to the tradition of this special local community, and any aggrieved individual could appeal to the sense of justice of his fellows to declare the "custom of the manor." These manorial courts adjudicated the son's inheritance of the father's rights to the land upon the payment of the customary "*gersum*" and "*heriot*," and saw him do his "fealty." They elected the *reeve* and the *hayward*, and took their oaths. They made the rules for the use of meadows. The manorial court governed the labor service, it punished trespass, protected the forest from depletion, presided over all transfer of land held in villeinage, and of free land under certain conditions. It regulated the serf's freedom to marry, to take orders, and to leave the manor. It took cognizance of offenses against morality, of certain minor cases of violence, of the driving away of a neighbor's cattle, or the carrying

[22] Quoted by H. S. Bennett: *Life on the English Manor* (Cambridge: Cambridge University Press; 1938), p. 203.

off of the village crops. Breaches of contract and failure to fulfill obligations, and even such personal matters as slander, came before the manorial court for public hearing and judgment.

The juries, elected by the courts, looked into matters touching the king's peace, and reported on clipping of coins, the haunting of taverns at night, the harboring of strangers, and all serious infringements of the law, such as theft, violence, and murder.[23]

The manorial court provided the serf with "the same justice as that which the freeman got; he got in theory the judgment, not of his lord, but of a body of doomsmen who were at least his peers." [24]

Custom ruled more than the economic and civil life of the community. It prescribed the social practices as well. It ruled the marriage bargain and in some places decided that only those should marry who were going to inherit their fathers' holding or acquire land in some other way. Nor was a man free to bequeath his holding except as local custom dictated. More than that, custom in parts of England seemed to require that a family holding should not be increased by acquisition or diminished by alienation. If the other children left the land, they took a portion of their father's property as their share; if they stayed, they were entitled to their keep, but they could not marry. The holding was preserved in the family. The unmarried members were cared for, but the property remained undivided and passed intact from generation to

[23] Ibid., pp. 217–18.
[24] Pollock and Maitland: *A History of English Law*, Vol. I, p. 593.

generation. If a man grew old and wished to have his land passed to his heir, he could do so, or if childless he could find an heir. In either case the beneficiary agreed to give the old folk who had surrendered their property the food and shelter they would need for the rest of their natural lives. The details differ from place to place, but the essential story remains the same.[25]

The manor village was a community in which all members took part. The customary rule governed the life of man from his cradle to his grave. It prescribed for the gleaning, plowing, and harvesting of crops and the keeping of animals, as well as for marriage, inheritance, church attendance, and church festivals. This village community, when it came before the king's courts, appeared not as composed of separate villagers, but as a community.

The men of the village were collectively responsible for all fines laid upon the community.[26] This was very different from what came to pass in the wake of the Industrial Revolution, and from the situation of slaves on colonial plantations. Here on the manor "all-powerful custom determined every man's rights and obligations." [27] And, "Just as each manor formed a jurisdictional unity, so also it formed a religious one. . . . Thus the manor was not only an economic but a social institution. It imposed itself upon the whole life of its inhabitants." [28]

[25] G. C. Homans: *English Villages of the Thirteenth Century* (Cambridge, Mass.: Harvard University Press; 1941), pp. 144–5.

[26] Ibid., p. 338.

[27] Henri Pirenne: *Economic and Social History of Medieval Europe*, p. 64.

[28] Ibid., pp. 63–4.

Membership in a guild, manorial estate, or village protected man throughout his life and gave him the peace and the serenity from which could flow the medieval art and craft. The life of man was a nearly unified whole. Being a member of an integrated society protected and raised the dignity of the individual, and gave each person his own special role. Each man, each act, was part of a total life drama, the plot of which was known and in which the part allotted to each was prescribed. No one was isolated or abandoned. His individuality and his ambitions were fulfilled within the customary law that ruled the community to which he belonged.

Man has always been a member of a "society," as the examples cited above help to demonstrate. These particular illustrations of this point are simply selected examples. They do not pretend to be complete studies descriptive of the complexities and contradictions of the various social systems from which they are taken. But these, and the thousands of other available illustrations, do establish the fact that man has always lived in a "society," possessed of a customary law and "governance" that gave each individual a part in a common drama.

The enclosures and the agricultural revolution, among other events and influences, destroyed the manorial court and undermined the rural village, while the changing conditions of the market and the difficulties of maintaining a limited monopoly weakened the guilds. Their final abolition by legal enactment, in France in 1776 and 1791, in England in 1814 and 1835, and later in Germany and other European countries, made a drastic change in the historically "normal" association among men working at similar tasks. The individualistic theory upon which the abolition of the guilds was justified denied the legitimacy of ancient ways among men. The early appearance of the trade-union, in spite of legal opposition, and its survival in the face of many obstacles merely reasserted an age-old experience—the moral fusion of men physically associated in labor. The need for creating a union that would express the identity of a group of men who, by working together, had found their own way of describing their part of the universe proved irreducible, imperative. The needs satisfied for so long by the village, manorial court, and guild now found expression in a different organization. But the ends to be served remained the same.

The attempt by the workers to achieve economic security for the individual and identity for the group in a complex and essentially unstable economy has provoked difficulties unforeseen by either the laborers or their employers. The role of the new union, which, it should be emphasized, is not derived from the guild, was to prove profoundly different because the economy within which it was establishing itself had greatly changed. And before the new organization of labor became strong enough to protect the worker in mine and factory, he suffered the evils that followed the destruction of the society within which man can live as a moral person.

CHAPTER III

The Destruction of the Community

THE VILLAGE, the manor, and the guild provided both a "society" and a way of life, which were little affected by the doings of kings and nobles. Centuries might pass and dynasties disappear, but the ways of the community remained much as they always had been. The changes that brought modern industry into being, however, destroyed the habits that had maintained an orderly community. In the earlier days "custom was the shield of the poor." The new factories, with their insistence upon an individual wage bargain, threw this precious heritage to the winds, and man found himself in a world without a definition of right respected by the whole community. What the Industrial Revolution did to the individual in general and to the laborer in particular was to disrupt his society and undermine the customary law he lived by. It threw him upon his own resources. Man was now "free" in a way he had never been previously. There had been unfortunate "masterless" men before, and itinerant tinkers and scholars, but here, for the first time, man in general was made independent. If he could get a job, he could live by himself, without a family, friends, guild, or craft.

The complex forces that wrought these changes are well known, but the long-run consequences of this loosening of the moorings were unforeseen. The weakening of the community adversely affected not only men, but also women and children, old and young, skilled and unskilled. Its effects reached all groups in the community, so that a society of traditional "status" melted away and became increasingly composed of isolated, equal, and independent individuals. For the first time men became responsible to themselves alone, and irresponsible for the well-being of anyone else, even their closest relatives. Even if this splintering of the community was never completed, because there is no absolute logic to a social movement except in theory, it still remains true that its effects were sufficiently broad to describe an age. It laid the basis for a series of political upheavals of which we in our own time are the unwitting heirs.

It was the payment of a money wage to each separate worker, man, woman, or child, that became the immediate cause of the breakdown of the older society. The payment of a money wage detached children from their parents and made old and young equal. By means of a separate money wage, the younger could be better off than their elders, and sons could lord it over their fathers. Under the new dispensation even daughters were free to abandon the family roof and live "independent" lives. Hordes of individual men, women, and children, drawn from other towns, and in the United States from different countries, were thrown together in city slums to find for themselves the key to the good life that had in the past been provided by the family, the church, the guild, and the community. The isolated worker, free and irresponsible, dominated the scene. A steel center such as Pittsburgh could be described as a city of single men, each of whom was free, independent, and equal. Every man was free if he had a job, independent because he could leave it, and equal because he had an opportunity to be measured by his ability to earn a living.

Equality for the worker took a new and strange form: the earning of a money wage. It came to mean equality for competitive strife. To secure a job and hold it proved to be the test of all else and the very means of survival. A kind of free-for-all became the prevailing rule among men, and the social milieu was sufficiently fluid to make room at the top for many who had the energy, skill, or shrewdness to swim with the tide and outstrip their opponents. But that was for the fortunate, the strong, and the ruthless. The mass of men found the going hard, the life a lonely one, and the boasted freedom something of a burden.

Many forces had helped bring these changes about: the enclosures, the discovery of America, the Reformation, the confiscation of the monastic estates, the commercial revolution, the civil wars in Great Britain, the mercantilist policy of the European powers, the agricultural revolution, the Enlightenment, the decline of the guilds, the increased use of machines, and the French Revolution.

All these had their part in shaping the Industrial Revolution and the individualism that characterized it.

In England the enclosure of the common fields had begun before the Tudors. The small holdings were encroached upon more or less irregularly until the middle of the eighteenth century, when rapid changes in farming methods greatly increased the pressure against the scattered field system of the peasantry. The improvement in roads and canals opened more distant markets for farm products. The new machines took weaving and spinning from the cottage to the factory, favoring the growth of towns. To improve the farmers' use of the land came to be very much the fashion, and was promoted by such people as Jethro Tull (1674–1741), and by Lord Townshend (1674–1738), known as "Turnip Townsend." It even attracted so elite a person as "Farmer George"—King George III. These reformers worked at improving crops, cattle, and ways of tilling the land. Their efforts were an evidence of, and contributory to, the changing of the English countryside.

Half of the parishes in England had open fields, and as late as 1700 there was still a vast extent of waste land, estimated by Gregory King at ten million acres. After that date 4,800 Parliamentary acts and awards made possible the enclosure of 6,500,000 acres, nearly one fifth of the whole country. So broad was this attack on the little holdings that in fourteen counties between a quarter and a half of the land was thus affected.[1]

[1] Herbert Heath, in *The Encyclopedia of the Social Sciences*, Vol. V, p. 525.

Equally significant was the enclosing of the waste. The twenty years from 1761 to 1781 saw the culmination of the long movement for the enclosing of the commons, and the forty-two years from 1802 to 1844 saw the same process of enclosure extended on a large scale to the waste lands.[2] Between them the enclosure of the commons and the waste effected a great change in the lives of the English people, who until then had lived close to the soil. The enclosures forced the people to abandon the land, increased their dependence upon money, an undermined the community in which they lived.

The manorial system had made little use of money. Dues and service were usually paid in labor and in produce. Money had not completely disappeared, but it was little used because the rural population had slight need for commerce and trade. There was not much movement of merchandise, and therefore small occasion for the circulation of money. The serf worked for his lord a stated number of days during the year and gave him a customary portion of the goods he made, such as linen and heavy woolen cloth. He might also give the lord some of the eggs, corn, chickens, lambs, and pigs he raised. It was not a money economy in spite of the few pence that had to be paid in addition to goods and service. It was an economy independent of the large markets, and found its well-being in its own products rather than in imported goods.[3] In fact, such medieval commerce as

[2] A. H. Johnson: "The Disappearance of the Small Landowner," *Ford Lectures* (Clarendon Press, 1909).

[3] Henri Pirenne: *Economic and Social History of Medieval Europe*, p. 142.

went on was little dependent upon local supplies. It was primarily an export and import trade, carried on by professional merchants. "Strange as it may seem, medieval commerce developed from the beginning under the influence not of local but of export trade." [4] The goods were of foreign origin, and "early medieval commerce bears a certain resemblance to colonial trade." [5]

Even with the disappearance of the manorial system typical of the Middle Ages, the life of the average peasant was largely independent of an income in money. His land, held in tenure freehold or copyhold, supplied him with the basic grain and root crops, and the commons and waste offered a variable and many-sided contribution to his real income. He had a right to graze his ox, and the ox was slaughtered, when old, and salted down for meat; the hide, tanned in the village, was available for a hundred different uses. The cow gave milk and was calculated to supply "seven stone of cheese and one stone of butter between May and Michaelmas." In its turn, when old it could give both meat and hide. The sheep, though more troublesome to maintain, gave wool, skins, carcasses, and even milk. The fact that the sheep was part of almost every peasant's stock is indicated by the village sheepherd, so commonly referred to in the literature of manor and village. The ubiquitous pig was invaluable and called for the existence of the village swineherd, as the geese called for the gooseherd. The chicken was in every yard and, in addition to providing meat, promised to lay a

[4] Ibid., p. 142.
[5] Ibid., p. 142.

hundred and twenty eggs and hatch seven chicks a year. The wastes and the forest provided wood for the fireplace, for construction of house and barns, for repair of farm buildings, for the making of the wagon, the plow, and the ox-yoke. They offered turf for roofing and, if necessary, for drying and burning for heat in the winter. The waste and the forest had birds and beasts that were snared and hunted for food, and the streams and lakes contained fish and eels to be caught and eaten or salted away for the barren winter months.[6]

These free and natural foods were lost to the peasant when the enclosure deprived him of access to the common and the waste. As late as 1660 the laboring population, in the main, was still attached to the land and still had the right to free, even if limited, use of what nature made available.[7] The enclosures affected more than the purely agricultural population. Every manor, every village, had people whose business was primarily handicraft and who had only a small holding in the land. But the holding gave them access to grazing rights in the commons and to use of the many resources of the wastes that surrounded every town and stretched beyond the limits of many a manor. Even "the weaving and spinning which went on in the cottages in the rural districts was at first secondary in importance to agricultural labor." [8] Village

[6] H. S. Bennett: *Life on an English Manor*, pp. 90–3. A. H. Johnson, op. cit., p. 116.

[7] Edgar S. Furniss: *The Position of the Laborer in a System of Nationalism* (Boston: Houghton, Mifflin Co.; 1920), p. 212.

[8] Hewins: *English Trade and Finance (1892)*, p. 94, quoted by Furniss, op. cit., pp. 212–13, Appendix I.

craftsmen had garden plots and their rights in the commons. "Alexander Carpenter held only a house and half an acre . . . Robert of the Mill . . . three acres." The carpenter built the carts, made the plows and harrows, and helped in the housing. The miller ground the grains. To these were added such people as "Adam Baker" and "Geoffrey Weaver," and the village rolls were full of names that reflected the local crafts: Draper, Comber, Napper, Tailor, Textor, Ironmonger, Tannur, Couper, and many others. They filled the village needs for specialized crafts and skills, but were not a people apart, and were not solely dependent upon a money wage for their income.[9] It was still customary to pay wages in kind, and even in 1795 there were counties in England where food "was a normal supplement to money wages." [10]

The enclosures changed the status of a people who from time out of mind had made their living by working the land. They knew but little of a money wage and even less of prices and markets. They lived by what they made themselves with their own hands, by what they grew on the land they tilled, by what their animals yielded, by what the streams, the forest, and the waste supplied. The upsetting of the traditional rights of the people to the land was defended upon grounds of efficiency and progress. The visible result was to deprive the villagers of their living and to force them to accept public charity if there was no job to be had or if the job did not pay enough. But as Arthur Young noted in 1801, ". . . they

[9] H. S. Bennett, op. cit., pp. 66–8.
[10] Edgar S. Furniss, op. cit., p. 209, Appendix I.

would rather have a cow than any parish allowance." [11]

These changes adversely affected the freeholder and the copyholder as well as the tenant who had no land of his own. With the enclosure of the commons and the waste they found the little piece of land they retained insufficient for their needs. They lost or sold their small holdings and joined the landless in the towns and cities. Those who had partially clothed and fed themselves, even when engaged in industrial crafts, now depended on a job for their money and on the store for their food.

With the worker's loss of his age-old claims upon the soil went his traditional rights and participation in the community. The disinherited laborer who had no job was forced upon the public rolls. The adoption of the Speenhamland system by the Berkshire magistrates in 1795 pauperized the English working class. It spread so widely over England that when it was abolished, in 1838, Northumberland and Durham were almost the only counties where the practice had not developed. The system was to supplement the wages of the worker according to the price of flour, so as to give him three shillings a week for himself and one and sixpence for his wife and each member of his family. The result was to demoralize the worker. He could now get help from the parish only if he was destitute, and unless he could get help, he could not get a job. The employer would not pay him a full wage so long as the town was prepared

[11] Arthur Young: *Applying Wastes* (1801), p. 14, quoted in Furniss, op. cit., p. 214, Appendix I.

to provide part of his needs from the public funds.

The position of the worker degenerated as his "society" disappeared, and the game, vagrancy, and settlement laws were made more stringent to keep the needy from poaching on the game or wandering from town to town. The means of livelihood had now passed out of the worker's own hands. "In one district it was the custom for the overseer to put up the laborers to auction every Saturday night: they were let generally at from 1*s*. 6*d*. to 2*s*. a week, and their provisions, their families being kept by the parish." [12]

The long process of the enclosure had now worked its full effects upon the people displaced from the land, and the new factory towns and cities into which they migrated were to add to their misery. The factory system, in its turn, proved to be both an economic and a social revolution. It added to the dissolution of the community and attacked the most intimate of human groupings, the family. The towns that grew up around the factories and mines provided little room for the ordinary decencies of life. In the older cities, such as Manchester and Birmingham, tradition and custom had some restraint upon the growing evil, but in the new towns, built about the mill or mine and located upon private land, there was neither urban experience to draw upon nor public policy to guide their development. In these communities the owner of the mine or factory frequently owned the houses the workers lived in as well as the store where they bought

[12] J. L. and Barbara Hammond: *The Rise of Modern Industry* (New York: Harcourt, Brace & Co., 1926), p. 96.

their food. By paying his laborers in token coin he reduced them to complete dependence. This occurred in spite of the fact that payment in token coin was against the law.

The community, in effect, had disintegrated. The family had all but disappeared. "Men, women and children of all sexes and ages are stowed away in bedrooms without curtains or partitions, it being no uncommon thing for nine or ten people not belonging to the same family to sleep together in one room." [13]

The houses crowded about the factory and mine, and the cities were overwhelmed by an increasing immigration from the rural districts. No parks were laid out, no sewage system was provided, and no street lighting was developed. "The streets are generally unpaved, rough, dirty, filled with vegetable and animal refuse, without sewers or gutters, but supplied with foul stagnant pools instead." [14] The busy factory town knew neither air, space, cleanliness, nor beauty. A comparison of some English towns in the sixteenth century and in the middle of the nineteenth throws the story into graphic relief:

Norwich had increased from 17,000 to 62,000 inhabitants, Leicester from 4,000 to 50,00, and Liverpool, a small village in the sixteenth century, had become a city of over 200,000 people. The gardens had disappeared, the courts had become crowded, the houses were so closely built that it was difficult to find a lane between them, and "in Liverpool, one-sixth of the people lived in 'under-

[13] J. L. and Barbara Hammond, op. cit., pp. 156–7.

[14] Frederick Engels: *The Condition of the Working Class in England in 1844* (London: Swan Sonnenschein & Co.; 1892), p. 26.

ground cellars.' "[15] The houses were overflowing, and in Norwich one often found ten persons to each room. Compared with three centuries earlier (1570), conditions had seriously worsened. There were then but 3.5 people per room.

A similar contrast can be drawn between the streets of the sixteenth and those of the nineteenth centuries. In the earlier days the local authority enforced cleanliness. Later no such power was exercised by the city officials. In the sixteenth century rubbish could not be thrown into the streets; in the middle of the nineteenth, "it was the accepted method of disposal." "In one town nearly 9,000 houses inhabited by 60,000 people were without ashpit, convenience, or one inch of ground on which to deposit filth, which therefore of necessity had to be thrown into the street. There was now no thought of inspection, and the sixteenth-century 'scavenger' with his cart would be useless, for the filth had become private property."[16]

The water system was inadequate; no public drainage was available. In the sixteenth century, in a small village, pig-keeping was regulated; in the middle of the nineteenth century "pigs, asses and poultry [were] kept in living houses," and many houses "were built with pigsties in the basement." "In Birmingham, in the middle of the nineteenth century, there were 1,600 pigsties." The pig that once had been banished from the community had

[15] J. H. Thomas: *Town Government in the Sixteenth Century* (London: George Allen & Unwin; 1933), pp. 167–70.

[16] Ibid., pp. 167–70.

returned three hundred years later "to become the scavenger."[17]

The improvement of the standard of living for the mass of the people, implicit in the Industrial Revolution, was not yet evident. Its immediate effects were baneful upon both the economic and the social position of the workers. The Industrial Revolution proved callous to human well-being, and in many instances made the family dependent upon its own children:

> "I hope you will get this Ten Hour Bill passed; I have two children, one seven and the other thirteen, at work at the factories, and I have not had the least stroke for"—I think he said—"the last thirteen months." He told me that they were earning seven or eight shillings a week, and he said, "That little girl has to go a mile and a half very early to her work, and she comes home at half-past eight, and all I see of her is to call her up in the morning, and send to bed, and it almost makes my heart break. We cannot get any work, and I know that I am living by the death of that child"; and he cried when he told me.[18]

The society of guild, manor, and village community had passed away. The individual workers, crowding the slums about the factories, had been reduced to indigence and degraded as men.

The new factories that worked this change in men's lives also stirred great hope for mechanical improvement

[17] Ibid., pp. 167–70.

[18] Quoted in Wing: *Evils of the Factory System*, p. 100. In J. L. and Barbara Hammond: *The Town Labourer, 1760–1832* (London: Longmans, Green & Co.; 1917), p. 32, footnote.

and economic progress. By a curious turn, however, the hope of improvement was not for the laborer. The workers' poverty and misery, it was said, were due to their own shortcomings. Their poverty was the natural result of their laziness and lack of thrift, but it was said to serve a good end. The indigence of the worker was considered necessary to social stability and economic progress.[19] Recreation was a waste of time, amusement was a sin, and rest was synonymous with idleness.

Pessimism over human destiny seemed natural to the age. Time and circumstances had combined to weaken the church and undermine the family. The crowded towns had demoralized the working people. Drunkenness and immorality had increased and become notorious. The tavern, with its profanity and its obscenity, became a conspicuous feature of urban life. Murder, robbery, and assault increased; the jails were crowded; and transportation and hanging were commonplace.

The new industrial society, so full of promise for the future, had little to offer in the way of immediate consolation. The doctrines of individualism proved a poor substitute for the older values. To the workers, individualism, in so far as they had heard of it, was just a word. It embodied no tradition and provided no comfort. To the workers, who needed succor the most, the new doctrine had least to offer. The workers required, as all men do, a society of which they were members and in which they played a role. They wanted, once again, an opportunity to act out their humble parts in some recog-

[19] Edgar S. Furniss, op. cit., p. 147.

nizable drama and to be members of some organized group. Without knowing it, they wanted to re-create a "society."

In 1800 there were many laws in opposition to the organization of the workers, but some of these were old and harked back to mercantilism. They were attempts to maintain the powers of the state in regulating industry. The newer Combination Laws of 1789 tried to free the rising industrialists from any interference by either the state or the workers. These acts made it a crime, not merely to strike for higher wages, but "by any means whatsoever to directly or indirectly decoy, persuade, solicit, intimidate, influence, or prevail. . . ." It was also a crime to refuse to work for another person, or to attend meetings, or to contribute to meetings that had it as their purpose to secure combination.[20]

In other words, personal isolation for the workers was to be accomplished by law, and, in effect, conversation between workers about their trade was subject to suspicion of conspiracy. The single magistrate, who had power to sentence a worker to three months in prison, was often a manufacturer himself. If that were not sufficient, outsiders were forbidden to aid any worker to attempt a reversal of the conviction.[21]

The social disintegration resulting from the destruction of the community by the enclosures and the urban slums in Great Britain was repeated in the United States by immigration. The classic study of what happened to the

[20] J. L. and Barbara Hammond, op. cit., p. 120.
[21] Ibid., p. 121.

Polish peasant when he migrated from his little rural community to the United States exemplifies the process, not merely for the Poles, but for all the peasant immigrants who poured into the growing American cities.[22] The story of family disruption, of the disappearance of the community, of overcrowding, of a disregard for life and limb, of child labor, was all reproduced upon the American scene. Here again was the loss of status and dignity incident upon the destruction of customary law and community identity:

> But it is in the immigrant lodging houses that conditions are worst. . . . Single men in groups of six to twenty go into one house in charge of a boarding-boss and his wife. . . . When the boarding-boss rents two rooms he and his wife sleep in the kitchen and the boarders take the other room. It is not unusual for the boarding-boss to rent but one room. He and his wife put their bed in one corner; the stove in another; and the boarders take the remainder. . . . Sometimes the rooms are so crowded that the boss and his wife sleep on the floor; and I repeatedly found cases where beds were being worked double shift—night and day.[23]

The conditions under which some immigrants made the transition from a rural village to an industrialized society is indicated in such accounts as this:

> Camp No. 17—The shanty consists of one room about 25 x 75. The bed stalls are arranged around the walls in

[22] W. I. Thomas and F. Znaniecki: *The Polish Peasant in Europe and America* (4 vols.; Boston: Richard G. Badger; 1918–20).

[23] P. Robert: "The New Pittsburghers," in *Pittsburgh Survey*, Vol. XXI, January 2, 1907.

three stories. Access to each row is obtained by a single movable step-ladder used in turn by the climbers. The floor is the bare ground, and has not been cleaned. . . . The shanty accommodates about 120 men. No provisions are made for toilet or washing, the neighborhood of the shanty being used for the former. There was no standing water; no dining room. The laborers eat mostly on flat stones arranged like tables on poles stuck in the ground.[24]

These things happen when a society natural to men working together disappears. When there is no community, there is no custom, rule, or law within which man can live in decency as a member of a society, and when the community disappears, the dignity of the worker as a human being declines.

[24] Edith Abbot: *Immigration, Select Documents and Case Records*, p. 487.

CHAPTER IV

Individualism and Social Theory

THE DISINTEGRATION of the community came at a time when the prevailing political and moral theory insisted that each man was endowed with equal rights. It also argued that every man, by himself, had all of the knowledge and wisdom required to make him the best judge of what was his own true interest. It gave each person credit for a true inner light by which he could tell the subtle distinctions between good and evil. It was always possible, and under the theory necessary, for the individual to do that which was best for him, and therefore best for society.

The economists strengthened the existing predisposition to individualism by saying that free economic bargaining between men would result in a harmony in which each would get his just due. Unconsciously, each in turn would contribute to the natural justice represented by all men working separately, each for his own interest. What the logic of the theory implied was that each man was sufficient unto himself, that the self-sufficient individuals were equal among themselves, and that among such equal individuals only a competitive relationship could reveal the perfect concord the design embodied. Government, therefore, rested upon each person and was derived from his consent. Morality, too, was completely personal, for on the principle of "pleasure and pain" only the inner man could be an adequate judge of what was good or evil. In economics the principle of gain and loss made each man the best judge of his role in the harmonious scheme.

This doctrine gave the social disintegration then taking place a moral purpose. The breaking down of customary and ancient "mysteries" that had clustered men together in small groups about some commonly held value was described as a good and progressive sign. In its extreme form the theory seemed to advance the idea that the best society was that in which organized human relations and responsibilities were least. One need but recall certain avowed implications of Malthusianism, the "tooth and claw" perversions of the theory of the survival of the fittest, and the widespread acceptance of the idea contained in Herbert Spencer's *Man versus the State.* The sum of the theory seemed to support the idea that man was related to the government vertically, each by himself, and to the society horizontally not at all. At most he was related to the society through his immediate family, which, however, was merely an extension of his own personality. Under those circumstances it was natural to believe that that government was best which governed least. If true harmony were to be found in the unimpeded competition between men, no other conclusion could be drawn.

The trend of events cast doubt not upon the theory of individual sufficiency, but upon the belief that that government was best which governed least. Some men looking about the world as it developed under the early impact of the Industrial Revolution were disturbed by what seemed to them the needless suffering resulting from the misuse of the government by the owners of industry. If that government was best which governed least, then to anarchists like Proudhon, who took the doctrine literally, that government was best which governed not at all, which removed itself from the scene and permitted the self-sufficient, morally competent individuals to work out the natural harmony, uncorrupted by legal interference.

That was one solution of the difficulty. The Socialists had another. They accepted the whole theoretical formula from Locke through Ricardo to Darwin plus Hegel. The individual was still equally endowed, but by controlling the government, some individuals, the propertied ones (called the *bourgeoisie*), oppressed the propertyless (called the *proletariat*). Each class was composed of individuals, and the ideal remained personal felicity. "To each the full product of his labor" was purely individualistic philosophy with a new bias. Under the new version that government was best which governed most. The present fault of government, the Socialists said, was that it as yet governed only to keep the rich in their possessions and the poor in their poverty.

The suggestion in the Socialist doctrine that the state will ultimately wither away is postponed to await the time when all men are truly equal. The belief in the equal endowment of all men is prerequisite to each variation of the formula that attempts to explain the rise of modern industry and its impact on society.

We thus have three solutions to this problem: that government is best which governs least; that government is best which governs not at all; and that government is best which governs most. The social-reform movements of the last hundred and fifty years in the Western World have quarreled mainly over the degree of public responsibility for individual felicity.

It is characteristic of the Industrial Revolution that each of the theories that accompanied it denied the community. The very idea of a "society" so congenial to the human being seemed to have evaporated, and philosophers talked about individual felicity as if it were to be found only in a social vacuum. Moreover, each of these theories assumes that the economic interest is the governing, perhaps even the exclusive, concern of the human being. By implication these theories deny the institutional structure of society. They assume that each person speaks for himself, unimpeded by the multiple influences that have shaped his values and provided him with moral and political ideals. In turn they all take individual perfectibility for granted and believe in felicity as the major end of life. This felicity is apparently to be had in isolation, outside any "society" where value and purpose derive from community tradition. In each of these theories, even in the Marxian conception of "to each the full product of his labor," there is the uncritical belief that men in pursuit of their own private ends will produce a self-perpetuating, free, and perfect world that will last forever. The perfect competition of the economist and the classless society of the Socialist both imply a static world. Once it was achieved, any disturbance would upset the ideal balance. It is revealing of more than the theory or the theorists to watch both the extreme individualist and the extreme communist aspire for the same goal, an individual felicity resting upon economic satisfactions and ending in so perfect a harmony that any movement would prove a disturbance. The ideal is quietude, perfect stillness—death.

All of these theories would relieve man from exercising any moral responsibility, for man can have a responsible role only in an imperfect world, a world of conflicting values and contradictory ends. Dissidence and stress are essential, not merely to a moral life, but to life itself. The desire of the theorist of the Industrial Revolution to escape from the real world is partly explained by the influences exercised upon the popular mind by the contemporary science of physics. The political theorist and the economist were deeply impressed by the breakdown of matter into atoms, and they proceeded to do the same to society. Men became interchangeable, equal, unrelated, and subject to manipulation. They ceased to be human. Morality and ethics disappear because they have no place among atoms, and the only force that keeps state and society from splintering is the selfish but equal economic motivation. That conception underlies both Bentham and Marx.

In addition to taking over the concept of the atom,

the social scientist also accepted the belief in a rational universe, governed by an inevitable law, and tried to apply it to the affairs of men. The laws were given, and all man needed to do was to discover them. The laws were inescapable: the law of diminishing returns, Malthus's law of population, the iron law of wages, and the theory of the survival of the fit. They were part of a universal system of law, the effects of which man could not avoid. If he were wise, he would accept the inevitable and submit. If he rebelled, the laws of nature would prove inexorable and reduce the foolish mortal to obedience. But the belief in law lends itself to both optimism and pessimism, to a beneficent and generous or a niggardly and harsh view of the universe. It was possible to assume that men always followed their own true interests, and that their infallible instincts always guided them aright. More than that, what each man did for his own good was also good for society as a whole. Locke, Adam Smith, Condorcet, and Bentham had a benevolent and kindly view of man, and in their hands he became a noble creature, judicious and wise in his ways. The great impediment to felicity was needless restraint, and associations that interfered with man's initiative were evil. The optimism of the philosophers, the increase in production, the flow of new inventions, and the growth of capital helped to convince politicians and preachers that a policy of nonintervention was best for the individual and for the state.

But the belief in a world governed by a universal law also served the pessimists. Ricardo and Malthus had a dour view of human nature. They could paint the destiny of man in somber colors and find wide acceptance because they too could argue that their doctrines were part of an inevitable natural law. To John Locke, it seemed that the "source of ideas every man has wholely in himself." [1] And "Everyone knows what his proper business is." [2] It therefore follows that "so far as a man has power to think or not to think, to move, or not to move, according to the preference or direction of his own mind, so far is a man free." [3]

To Adam Smith, this freedom was beneficent because "the study of his own advantage naturally, or rather necessarily leads him to prefer that employment which is most advantageous to the society." [4] The man who follows his interests "is in this, as in many other cases, led by an invisible hand to promote an end which was no part of his intention. . . . By pursuing his own interest he frequently promotes that of the society more effectually than when he really intends to promote it." [5]

According to Ricardo, however, the same invisible hand worked very different results. High wages encourage "the increase of population . . . wages again fall to their natural price," and "the condition of the laborers is most wretched." [6] There is nothing to be done

[1] John Locke: *Philosophical Works* (London: George Bell & Sons; 1905), Vol. I, p. 205.

[2] Ibid., p. 32.

[3] Ibid., p. 365.

[4] Adam Smith: *The Wealth of Nations* (London: Methuen & Co.; 1922 edition), Vol. I, p. 419.

[5] Ibid., p. 421.

[6] David Ricardo: *The Principles of Political Economy and Taxation* (New York: E. P. Dutton & Co.; 1911), p. 53.

about it because these "are the laws by which wages are regulated" and wages "should never be controlled by the interference of the legislature." [7]

To Malthus, the case is even more evident and the consequence calamitous: "Nature will not, nor cannot, be defeated in her purposes. . . . We cannot lower the waters of misery by pressing them down in different places." [8] The only remedy is to keep down the population, and for that Malthus argues that "Instead of recommending cleanliness to the poor we should encourage contrary habits. In our towns we should make the streets narrower, crowd more people into the houses, and court the return of the plague. In the country, we should build our villages near stagnant pools, and particularly encourage settlements in all marshy and unwholesome situations. But above all, we should reprobate specific remedies for ravaging diseases." [9]

That such should have been the policy recommended in all seriousness by a widely read and influential economist is explainable only because the very concept of a community governed by customary law had disappeared. As Bentham expressed the idea:

> The community is a fictitious body, composed of the individual persons who are considered as constituting as it were its members. The interest of the community then is what?—the sum of the interests of the several members who compose it.

[7] Ibid., p. 61.

[8] T. R. Malthus: *Principles of Population* (London: John Murray; 1826), Vol. II, pp. 300–1.

[9] Ibid., pp. 301–2.

> It is vain to talk of the interests of the community, without understanding what is the interest of the individual. A thing is said to promote the interest, or to be for the interest, of an individual, when it tends to add to the sum total of his pleasures: or, what comes to the same thing, to diminish the sum total of his pains.[10]

The prominence given to economic motives seemed to justify the process of social disintegration. As long as man followed his "economic interests," every other need would automatically fulfill itself. The fact that the pursuit, or seeming pursuit, of economic ends also led to social disintegration was unnoticed. Men without a stable family and a secure membership in a society can have no moral personality, and therefore no moral status. The theory of individualism was a great success in terms of immediate economic "progress," but it was at the expense of both the individual and of the society that gave man his reason for living. It was achieved at the expense of those responsibilities and values which made him a member of a society and therefore a man.

[10] Jeremy Bentham: *Principles of Morals and Legislation* (London: Clarendon Press; 1823), p. 3.

CHAPTER V

The Re-Creation of the Community

THERE is no simple logic to a broad economic and political movement. Thus, while prevailing theory and public policy were preoccupied with the expanding individualism, another and unheralded movement came into being. This new movement denied the theory without repudiating it and, where it could, counteracted in its own way the process of atomization.

As the Industrial Revolution became more inclusive, more and more individuals had to depend upon a wage-paying job, and their helplessness in relation to it increased. It was not theirs to keep and to hold. As business enterprises grew larger, contact between the worker and his employer became less frequent, and the opportunities for understanding and identity between the two decreased. A new phase in the structure of the economy had developed. The factory system contained numerous individually helpless persons, each dependent upon a common employer. Men were not competent to assert either moral or economic influence upon the conditions of their labor, or to influence the retention of their jobs. They were individually helpless, and equal in their helplessness.

What the workers had in common was their employer, the industry they worked in, the hours they labored, the bench or the machine they worked at, the wage rate they received, the foreman who ruled over them, the materials they worked with, the whistle that called them from their beds in the morning or brought a halt to their labors. In addition, they had each other in common. They worked together at the same bench, inside the same mill or mine, struggled with the same refractory materials, and were dependent upon one another's co-operation. Here was a new social factor. The same process that had gathered these laborers together had forged a "society" in which a sense of identity became inevitable. Their personal helplessness was apparent to each. Their collective strength was yet to be revealed, but it could be discovered in the fact that they were all equally dependent upon the power that had brought them together. Their mutual association and experience, their similar skills, their relationship at the work bench, the tools they used, and the materials with which they worked gave them a common language. They acquired the language of the craft, the job, the shop, and the industry. They shared the special points of pride and shame that can have only specific and local meaning. They could complain about light and heat, or cold and dampness. They could indulge in interminable talk about the job, infinitely interesting in its repetitious monotony because it detailed the daily round of the little things men share. It gave them a common, if local, vocabulary. The employer became the catalytic agent that crystallized them into a self-conscious group. When a conflict stirred, this provided the stimulus to bring it to the surface.

Thus the social atomization resulting from the payment of an individual money wage was in time to be defeated by the fusing of men together functionally, and this functional coalescence became the firm foundation upon which the trade-union movement grew, and which, in fact, made it inevitable.

The original organizer of the trade-union movement is the shop, the factory, the mine, and the industry. The agitator or the labor leader merely announces the already existing fact. This is true in spite of the many instances of workers refusing to join a union. The process has gone on for so long a time, and over so wide an area, that it must be looked upon as an organic phenomenon, naturally following the spread of modern industry. The union is the spontaneous grouping of individual workers thrown together functionally. It reflects the moral identity and psychological unity men always discover when working together, because they need it and could not survive without it. There is nothing new about this. The fact that it takes the form of a trade-union is a historical accident, determined by the type of association the machine imposes. The theory which insisted that labor was a commodity like any other made collective action the only means of asserting the moral status of the individual. The trade-union was the visible evidence that man is not a commodity, and that he is not sufficient unto himself.

The emergence of the union was always on a local basis and was generally unpremeditated. It had no long-range plan, was often "provoked" by the breaking of some unwritten rule that had grown up in the relationship between "master" and "man," and had immediate and specific ends only. In their origin local trade-unions were spontaneous little democracies, constructing their own instruments of government out of their own experience. They were unstable in form, changeable in character, and characterized by an equalitarian bias. Composed of simple, hard-working men, little given to literary pursuits, the original members wrote their own rules in the homely language of simple folk. They chose their chairman for each meeting and often expected each man to take his turn in filling the formal duties of secretary and committee member. They taxed themselves a few cents a week or a month to cover their elementary needs, and found among their own members some honest fellow to act as treasurer. The officers were unpaid, and labored at their union duties after the day's work at the factory was done.[1]

In its origin the trade-union was a direct democratic grouping, but as the locals multiplied and as workers in a number of towns and cities in the same trade were organized, a representative government developed. This

[1] Cf. Sidney and Beatrice Webb: *Industrial Democracy* (London: Longmans, Green, & Co.; 1920), pp. 3–37.

consisted of elected delegates from all the locals, who then held regular meetings. In earlier days this larger organization, like the local trade-union, was unstable in form. Its officers, except perhaps for the secretary and treasurer, were unpaid. Its powers were limited by lack of funds, local jealousies, and inexperienced officers. It took a long time for organized labor to develop experienced officers, an enforcible system of taxation, and a body of constitutional law and working rules that could bind the local into a cohesive group. Many national trade-unions came into being only to be wrecked on the stubborn will of the locals which resisted or feared dictation from a central organization. In our industrial society, across the years, thousands of these little democracies arose and passed away. Some were destroyed by internal dissension, some by poor leadership, some by changing industrial conditions, some by opposition from the state, and some by the opposition of the owners of industry.

In the century-and-a-half-old history of trade-unionism in western Europe, England, and the United States, persistent, even if sporadic and in some measure hidden strife has permeated the relations between employers and trade-unions. Most of the conflicts have been local and unplanned, but the democratic ways of the early trade-union have fallen victim to this continuing war. The unions either were destroyed or have been compelled in many instances to sacrifice some of their local self-government to the demands of an endless battle with the employers.

The local and to a greater degree the national union

could survive only by developing leaders able to impose their authority, even if by autocratic and violent methods. On the American scene, violence has played an important part in the union struggles against recalcitrant workers as well as between employers and unions. Employers in the United States used violence, frequently on an organized scale. They took advantage of local, state, and federal laws. The courts were friendly to them because the law followed a doctrine of conspiracy and applied the injunction with increasing frequency in labor disputes. Some employers, in addition, hired the Pinkerton and Burns detective agencies and other strike-breaking groups that made organization difficult, expensive, and dangerous. The larger corporations, such as the steel companies, engaged a private police force against the developing trade-unions.

In some industries, especially coal and steel, the effort to organize the workers entailed so much violence that it carried the fervor of a private but armed crusade. If at present, as some complain, national and international unions in the United States are centralized and dictatorial it is because they rose to power in the midst of armed conflict. The strife was long and bitter because American experience had strengthened the belief in extreme individualism. The leaders of industry, until the day before yesterday at most, were convinced that trade-unionism was an evil to be resisted to the bitter end. Even after years of federal legislation favoring trade-unions, the hope still survives that American public opinion will one day turn against organized labor. How else explain the spending of "close to a million dollars for private detectives" by General Motors, between January 1934 and July 1936, in an effort to stave off organization of its workers? [2] Similarly, the Chrysler Corporation paid the Corporations Auxiliary Company over $61,600 in 1933, over $76,000 in 1934, and over $72,000 in 1935.[3] The desire to hamper trade-union organization was strong in the automobile industry, but no more so than in others.

American history is replete with attempts to prevent the growth of organized labor. It was part of the industrial scene for many generations, and persisted after the passage of the National Labor Relations Act.[4] Testimony before the La Follette Committee suggested that there were two hundred agencies in the United States engaged in labor espionage, employing over forty thousand operatives and spending many millions of dollars.[5] The Governor of Kentucky asserted that the coal operators in Harlan County maintained a reign of terror, controlled the police force and sheriff's office, intimidated ministers of the gospel, and suppressed free speech and free assembly, all in an effort to prevent unionization of

[2] Dixon Wechter: *The Age of the Great Depression* (New York: Macmillan Co.; 1948), p. 111.

[3] *Hearings before the Committee on Labor and Public Welfare.* U.S. Senate, 80th Congress, 1st Session, on S. 55 and S.J. Res. 22, Part 3, February and March 1947 (hereafter referred to as "*Hearings, I*"), p. 1314, "Progress Report of the Chairmen to the Members of the Special Committee to Study Problems of American Small Business."

[4] *Hearings before the Subcommittee on Education and Labor.* 74th Congress, 2nd Session on S. Res. 266, April 10–23, 1936. *Hearings of the La Follette Committee*, pp. 2–3, "Statement of J. Warren Madden, Chairman, National Labor Relations Board."

[5] Ibid., pp. 5–6, "Statement of Heber Blankenhorn, National Labor Relations Board."

their mines.[6] To carry on their war against organized labor, some of the steel companies equipped their private guards with riot guns, gas masks, shells, and gas grenades.[7]

These more recent practices are but a continuation of an older habit. A report on the steel strike of 1919 commented:

> The charges brought against the State Constabulary, Deputy Sheriffs, and Company police, deal with the murder of men and women—one as he was in his own yard—and the wounding of hundreds of others; the clubbing of hundreds; the assaulting of men while lawfully and peacefully pursuing errands on the streets, and of prisoners while they were locked in their cells; the arresting and holding of men and women for long periods in the jails and police stations without provocation, and even without definite charges being lodged against them . . . the frequent surrender of law and its administration by the public authorities to the local company officials.[8]

The steel companies subverted public authority and controlled public opinion because many local officials were also employees of the companies. The evidence here cited is but a fraction of the story. The full tale fills volumes of testimony before Congressional hearings, thousands

[6] "Report of Governor Laffoon's Investigating Committee," ibid., pp. 136–40.

[7] "Testimony of Heber Blankenhorn, of the National Labor Relations Board," ibid., p. 48.

[8] Committee of Inquiry, Interchurch World Movement: *Public Opinion and the Steel Strike* (New York: Harcourt, Brace & Co.; 1921), p. 177.

of pages in American newspapers, innumerable briefs before American courts, and is told in hundreds of pamphlets and books. Even so, the written record is incomplete, for most of the tale is buried in the suffering and hardship endured by thousands of workers in the New England cotton mills, the fruit farms of California, the mines of Colorado, and the forests of Washington and Oregon. There is probably no industrial locality in all of the United States where this long story of bitter and sometimes bloody conflict over the right to organize cannot be told in its own special detail.

But the effort of the workers to achieve organization went on, despite many defeats. In the nature of the case, it had to go on. The common needs of men thrown together and molded into a society by common experience had to find a vehicle. Under the circumstances, that vehicle could only be the union. The helpless individual could find neither dignity nor security in isolation, and the opposition and violence were in the end mere incidents in the inevitable coalescing of a society in which man could find himself a member of a community once again. Otherwise the whole history of modern labor unions would have no meaning, certainly no moral significance. It would have to be explained, as it often has been by its opponents, as a conspiracy. But the historical records show it to have been, over and over again, a spontaneous, unorganized assertion of a common purpose, by men who asked only for what they had to have if they were to remain men: recognition as members of a society, a fellowship in common duress—men organized for some common relief because no individual could alleviate the hardship that lay heavily upon them all, upon the society as a whole, in fact.

Spontaneous groupings and resistance to atomization were a necessary response to the rules that denied that men working together were a "society." The painful history of labor proved otherwise, and long before the powerful trade-unions impressed themselves upon the modern scene, the sudden rebellions of "unorganized" workers foreshadowed the theme that has since unfolded.

> I suspect from my reading of old English material, even of the eighteenth century, that you can have trade unionism without any trade unionists being aware of it; that the mores and codes of trade unionism can develop without formal organization. Even in the days when trade unions were not very strong, were loosely organized, and when only minorities of the workers joined and paid dues, workers, whether members or not, often operated in some respects as if they belonged to very compact societies.[9]

In the United States the same story repeats itself. There are long years of sporadic rebellions, evidencing the existence of a society with common mores. "Prior to 1797, the only recorded strikes of any workmen were 'unorganized,' and, indeed, such were the majority of the strikes that occurred prior to the decade of the thirties in the nineteenth century." [10] American trade-union his-

[9] Jacob Viner: "The Role of Costs in a System of Economic Liberalism," from *First 1947 Economic Institute* (Washington, D.C., 1947), p. 24.

[10] J. R. Commons: *History of Labour in the United States* (2 vols.; New York: Macmillan Co.; 1918), Vol. I, p. 109.

tory is filled with innumerable instances of workers going on strike without organization, without formalized leadership, without funds, and without support from any outside source. In Fall River, Massachusetts, in 1850, the spinners struck against a reduction in wages "without notice or consultation among themselves." [11] It has been estimated that in the fifty years before 1936 there were six thousand strikes in the textile industry, most of them without formal trade-union organization.[12]

Some of these "spontaneous strikes" lasted for months, attracted nation-wide attention, and were accompanied by considerable violence. Similar labor uprisings took place in the other industries—coal, steel, transport, clothing, and so on. In fact, the history of American trade-unionism is in some degree a history of "unorganized," unsupported, and unsuccessful strikes. Certainly most of them were local in origin, locally fought out, and independent of any national or international federation.

In Great Britain local friendly societies were started, broken up, and started again many times, long before an attempt to amalgamate these clubs into some cohesive organization was begun. The first friendly society of cotton-spinners in Stockport was founded in 1792, and only in 1810 was amalgamation attempted.[13]

National unions in the United States were not success-

[11] N. J. Ware: *The Industrial Worker* (Boston: Houghton Mifflin Co.; 1924), p. 116.

[12] *Hearings, I*, p. 1520, "Statement of George Baldanzi, Executive Vice President, Textile Workers' Union of America, C.I.O."

[13] J. L. and Barbara Hammond: *The Skilled Labourer, 1760–1832* (London: Longmans, Green & Co.; 1919), p. 93.

fully established until after the Civil War, and they remained few in number for many years. The idea of a national federation of labor was agitated by the machinists and blacksmiths at their convention in November 1860. In 1869 the secretary of the trade assembly at Louisville sent a letter to the trade-union organizations in the United States and Canada suggesting a national federation. The purpose of this federation was stated to be the "final abolition of strikes, and the establishment of trade agreements." That is the important point, for the Wagner Act is perhaps chiefly significant for substituting an election for a strike in an attempt to make possible a sufficiently stable organization with which "trade agreements" could be concluded. It must always be remembered that the great battle has been for recognition of the organization—that is, for the formalized "society," in which rules, laws, and traditions can have their acknowledged place and in which individual members can play their part in the drama. Without recognition there can be no formalized society, no accepted drama to act out, and no responsibilities for the individual or for the society to which the individual is functionally and organically related. That is why the battle for recognition of the workers' organization has been unending and why it has been resisted.

It has been resisted because a society tends to become all-embracing and a way of life. With organization achieved, the very nature of the trade-union movement changes, even if both workers and employers are unaware of the change and even if it takes a long time for the change to become apparent. With organization achieved and the union incorporated in the body politic as a going concern, representing the needs of the society of functionally grouped workers, it ceases to be primarily an instrument of war, and becomes an instrument of "governance," as all institutions are in their special province.

The ways of governance are infinitely variable and contradictory. In the long run, they can be dealt with only by patience and compromise, for compromise is the essence of wisdom and practicality in governance. But the trade-union movement cannot take on the characteristics of an institution until its right to exist and function ceases to be a matter of dispute or of doubt. Like all institutions, it eventually tends to be accommodated within the larger community and assumes responsibilities not merely for itself but for the community. It is in the nature of a going institution to speak for the whole community even when it is arguing its own case, but this identification with the whole must wait for the end of the war over the right to exist. Only when the battle for recognition is finished can the institutional role come into its own. If the trade-union could not fulfill its larger institutional responsibilities, it would have no reason for existence, would not be a true society, would have no moral role, and would disintegrate.

In the long run the trade-union movement can survive as a unique society, resting upon a functional grouping, only if it fulfills the manifold duties of any institution, which are to serve and protect its members, whom it conceives to be the entire community. No institution has survival value unless it conceives of itself as exercising a necessary moral role for the whole of society, and this moral role includes the economic, political, social, and other interests of man.

It is for this reason that the Wagner Act is important. Not only did it facilitate the organization for which labor has fought these many years, but it has also eased the maturing of a society essential to industrialism. Experience and time will teach and discipline the trade-union movement, and it will ultimately develop a tradition and unwritten law that will describe its responsibilities as well as its prerogatives.

The shift in policy toward trade-union organization, represented by the Wagner Act, is not something imposed by the New Deal and the Great Depression. It is primarily a change in the composition of American labor. The enormous migration between the Civil War and the First World War made the effort to organize the workers in the United States peculiarly difficult. Employers took advantage of the new immigrants to defeat strikes and disrupt established trade-unions. The history of labor unions in steel, textiles, and coal is an unhappy tale of the use of helpless and uninitiated immigrants to prevent the establishment of trade-unions.

This, too, explains the long campaign of American labor to restrict immigration. The flood of workers from abroad repeatedly overwhelmed the unions. It is also true that in special instances the immigrants proved to be neither docile laborers nor willing instruments against the unions. There are innumerable instances of immigrants supplying the leadership for successful trade-unionism. Samuel Gompers, Sidney Hillman, David Dubinsky, and Philip Murray were all born abroad, and they are merely conspicuous instances of a host of labor leaders who came from across the ocean.

This is one side of the story. There were also successful industrialists, such as Andrew Carnegie, who helped remake the industrial scene in the United States. He, too, like thirty-eight million others between 1820 and 1940, was an immigrant who came to seek his fortune and make his home in the New World.

The conspicuous exceptions merely illumine the anonymous men who were caught up in a strange world where thousands of them unwittingly fought the battle of the employers against the attempt to organize American labor.[14]

Equally, if not more, significant was the gap between the European peasant and the American industrial worker who belonged to a labor union. Their vastly different experiences and outlooks were worlds apart. The effort to convert a newcomer from a rural district in some European country, and to endow him with the psychology and the values normal to workers in a modern factory was

[14] "The enormous immigration of 1880–1884 facilitated the efforts of employers to obtain immigrants as strikebreakers and wage levelers. Large numbers of immigrants were imported from Europe to work at wages below those American union labor received. The Knights of Labor led the movement in the 'eighties to obtain legislation prohibiting the immigration of contract laborers, and the anti-contract labor law passed by Congress on February 2, 1885, was due almost entirely to their efforts." J. R. Commons, op. cit., Vol. II, p. 19.

both baffling and heartbreaking, and proved almost more than the American trade unionists could accomplish. To add to the differences in habits and attitudes between a peasant and a factory laborer, there was the additional difficulty of multiple and mutually unintelligible languages.[15]

In 1910, immigrants represented 48.3 per cent of those employed in coal mining, 65.4 in copper mining, and 66.8 in iron mines. In the clothing industry over 70 per cent of the white males were immigrants. In bakeries, tanneries, woolen and worsted mills, blast furnaces, and rolling mills over 50 per cent were immigrants. In slaughterhouses, car and railroad shops, breweries, brass mills, carpet mills, silk mills, and rubber factories and in the construction of streets, roads, sewers, and bridges they made up over 40 per cent of all white males employed.[16]

It is no wonder that labor organizers despaired of achieving effective trade-unionism while half or more of the workers in the basic industries were recently arrived peasants, speaking many different languages. How great was the burden of converting the foreign-born worker into a good American trade-unionist can be seen from the cultural variety and complexity that has to be dealt with by the Catholic Church in the United States:

[15] "Labor organizations are handicapped by the mixed nationalities, languages and religions which make it impossible even to bring them together on a mutual understanding." Ibid., p. 24.

[16] United States Bureau of the Census, Thirteenth Census of the United States, Population Vol. IV. A. Ross Eckler and Jack Zlotnick: "Immigration and the Labor Force," from *The Annals of the American Academy of Political and Social Science*, March 1949.

The Directory (January 1, 1947) lists some 2,000 parishes as being Armenian, French, German, Polish, Syrian, or of other nationalities and rites. Other sources indicate that at least 2,855 parishes are serving Catholics of Armenian, Assyrian, Belgian, Carpatho-Russian, Chinese, Croatian, Czech, Dutch, French, German, Hungarian, Italian, Lithuanian, Maltese, Polish, Portuguese, Rumanian, Russian, Slovak, Slovene, Spanish (Mexican and Puerto Rican), Syrian and Ukrainian origin. Most of them are of Roman Catholic rite. A few hundred belong to the Armenian, Byzantine (Greek), Chaldean, Maronite, and Melchite rites. Among those of the Byzantine rite is the Ukrainian diocese having 138 Ukrainian parishes with 307,065 members. The so-called Pittsburgh diocese includes 165 Carpatho-Russian, 15 Hungarian, and 2 Croatian parishes with some 285,652 members. Assuming that these figures are typical, the total number of Catholics belonging to known non-English or nationality parishes exceeds five million. Another five million in all probability belong to nationality parishes although the latter are not identified as such.[17]

The problem of the numerous languages spoken by American immigrants is further illustrated by the fact that 973 newspapers in 40 languages were being published in the United States at the end of July 1948.[18]

This illustrates the situation as it is today. The story in 1910, if it were to be detailed, would be even more

[17] Yaroslav J. Chyz and Read Lewis: "Agencies Organized by Nationality Groups in the United States," from *The Annals of the American Academy of Political and Social Science*, March 1949.

[18] Ibid., pp. 155–6.

impressive. But by 1936, when the Wagner Act was enacted, a generation had passed since the flood of immigrants, with their multiple languages and rural habits, had been sharply halted by the Immigration Act of 1917 and the Quota Act of 1921. By 1936, the majority of industrial workers were American-born and reared in the American tradition.

Those who blame the New Deal and the Wagner Act for the increasing power of American trade-unions give too much weight to the influence of politics on the growth of American labor organization. The New Deal merely hastened the process. It neither initiated it nor could have prevented it. The influences responsible for the rapid growth of our trade-unions are those that converted the immigrant's children into Americans, educated them in public schools, taught them the English language, endowed them with the precious American heritage of independence and with the traditional American technique of democratic gathering for the discussion of common difficulties. It was inevitable that American-trained and educated workers, thrown together in the factories, should meet together and attempt to deal with their needs as a group. They brought their individualism, their ambition, and their desire for progress and improvement into the factory. The factory converted them into a "Society," with a sense of cohesive interdependence. Here they applied their American-derived mores and skills, their experiences with the gang, fraternal orders, baseball teams, and Rotary clubs, to the task of meeting the needs imposed by modern industry.

More significant than the numerical growth in trade-union membership is the increasing range and variety of occupations now included in trade-unions. We had actors' and musicians' unions before the New Deal. Now we have trade-unions formed by lawyers working in large firms,[19] by professional teachers of dancing,[20] and by plant guards, whose right to organize has been upheld by the Supreme Court.[21]

If the trend of the times is still insufficiently indicated, it needs only to be added that employees of the New York Stock Exchange, the Curb Exchange, and banks, have recently formed trade-unions. Adding meaning to the need for a union, as representing those elements of the new "society" which can be represented by no other contemporary agency, foremen in industrial plants have organized unions, and their right to do so has also been upheld by the Supreme Court.[22]

The complex social forces on the American scene, among which the Depression, the New Deal, and the Wagner Act are but surface phenomena, had made some fifteen million American workers members of trade-unions by 1948. What began as a weak attempt to discover a voice for expressing the needs of the new society has, in the course of a century, become a great movement. This is the unforeseen answer to the effort to dissolve the society as a conspiracy, and to insist, as Bentham did, that

[19] *New York Times*, January 29, 1948.

[20] Ibid., May 7, 1947, "Pickets from Conga Line. 200 Dance in a Demonstration Outside Arthur Murray Studio."

[21] Ibid., May 20, 1947.

[22] Ibid., March 11, 1947.

the "community is a fictitious bond." This, too, is the answer to the theory that each individual stands in a competitive position to every other except perhaps by the quaint quality, as Adam Smith put it, of "truck and barter," which distinguishes man from the beasts of the field.

It would be a mistake to assume that the trade-unions were alone in their repudiation of the doctrine that each man stands by himself. That belief was also denied by others. The philosophers and economists of individualism never had it all their own way. There were opponents from the beginning, and there is a great tradition of humanism and compassion in European and American politics, philosophy, and law, which counters, at first ineffectively, the driving forces operating for the atomization of society and the isolation of man. That tradition in England includes such names as Cobbett, Shaftesbury, Romilly, Dickens, Byron, Coleridge, Carlyle, Ruskin, Charles Kingsley, and many others. It also includes popular movements, such as Christian Socialism, friendly societies, consumers' co-operatives, mechanics' schools, Sunday schools, and Methodist chapels.[23]

These and many similar movements were part of a social and political milieu that in 1802 led to the limitation of the hours of labor for children under twelve, and

[23] I do not include the social revolutionists, for they had no place for compassion, and no interest in the naturally constructive and humane reaction to the evil and suffering the Industrial Revolution produced. To them the evils were useful because they could be exploited for revolutionary purposes, so as to escape, not so much from these current evils, but by some magic, hidden in a verbal formula, to achieve a world where evil and dissidence would find no place.

the prohibition of night work for children. In 1816 transportation of children was prohibited; in 1819 children under nine were prohibited from working in factories. This remedial legislative program has continued uninterrupted and has spread to industrial countries all over the world. The International Labor Office and the New Deal are merely aspects of the trend to place protective legal devices about the individual and to soften the harsh impact of industrialization by enforcing minimum standards.

These changes in governmental policy are of lesser import, however, than the growth of the trade-union movement. The trade-union saved the worker his initiative and gave him an opportunity to act as a moral person. The "society" that he needed had returned. He was a man once again, not just a cog in a machine, and not just a "hand" to be discarded and abandoned.

CHAPTER VI

Trade-Unionism and the Utopians

THE TRADE-UNION movement, in spite of its profoundly creative role in the modern world, has had few friends among the intellectuals, and some of those avowed friends were, and are, its worst enemies. The future historian, pondering the complexities of the last two hundred years, will be intrigued by the failure of the intellectuals to recognize the importance of trade-unionism as a force reshaping our industrial world. Most of the intellectuals of the period have sought to escape from their own society, either by trying to cast it in a form that it could not take, or by attempting to destroy the basis upon which it rested and to rebuild it upon a new foundation.

The classical economists and their disciples belong to the first group; the Socialists, the Communists, and their various sects, to the second. Neither could accept trade-unionism as a creative and enduring social force reshaping the economic structure and redefining the place of man within it. The classical economists denied significance to the trade-union except as an impediment to the beneficent workings of unrestricted competition.

To them the trade-union movement was either useless because it could bring no improvement to the workers, or harmful because it created artificial monopolies, higher costs, and needless restriction upon the natural mobility of labor in an otherwise free market. While the classical economists denied either its necessity or its usefulness, the Socialists and the Communists denied the trade-union's importance except as a possible tool for their own revolutionary purposes. Neither group could recognize that it was faced with an economic, social, and political metamorphosis. The classical economists wished to make manifest the natural harmony by removing every hindrance. The Socialists and Communists wished to evoke their own peculiar social harmony by reshaping society to their hearts' desire. If they could not use the trade-union movement as a tool for the achievement of that dream, they, too, found it recalcitrant and obstructive.

To the economist, the trade-union's efforts were needless, because, as McCulloch put it, "It is impossible for the employers of labor artificially to reduce the rate of wages." [1] They were also harmful, because they tampered with nature's immutable laws. Labor could not improve its position, because "Nature's violated laws vindicate their authority by a sure reaction. The presumptuous mortal, who dares to set his selfish will against divine ordinances, brings on his head inevitable retribution; his

[1] J. R. McCulloch: *A Treatise on the Circumstances which Determine the Rate of Wages and the Condition of the Labouring Classes* (London, 1851), pp. 489–99.

momentary prosperity disappears, and he pays in prolonged suffering, the penalty of his suicidal success." [2]

While the economists decried trade-unionism as a wasted effort, the Socialists and Communists sought to capture the workers' organizations and imbue them with a special purpose. Otherwise the trade-unions would impede their hope of the "revolution" and the harmonies that lay just beyond. The difference between the Socialists and the Communists on the one hand and trade-unions on the other is part of the substance of our society and cannot be bridged. The Socialists and Communists operate with general ideas, and are given over to large plans for the establishment of social "harmony," but the trade-union movement seemed to have no rational basis. It lacked a doctrinal foundation. It had no theory, and it offered no explanation of the beginning and the end of things. It was as perplexing and as self-renewing as life itself, and it was internally contradictory. It had no sense of direction. Its arguments—if so they could be called—were sentimental and emotional. It appealed to values the revolutionists repudiated, and, worst of all, it merely sought to improve the position of the workers here and now.

The chagrin of the Communists today and the Socialists yesterday is, and was, caused by the lack of logic and rationality of the trade-unions. Lacking a body of simple doctrine, they surely lacked truth. The trade-unionist, in the eyes of both the Socialists and the Communists,

[2] James Stirling: *Trade Unionism*, p. 36. Quoted in Sidney and Beatrice Webb, op. cit., p. 616.

was a promoter of treason to the great obsession of our times: a revolution that would usher in a perfect world, composed of perfect men. The social revolutionaries, therefore, had the alternative of destroying the trade-union movement or attempting to capture it and endow it with unifying ideas that would make it serve the revolutionaries' own ends. They would, as the Communists have done, use it and then emasculate it.

The revolutionaries could not recognize that the trade-union movement embodied a changing industrial society. They could not see that the quarrel between the labor union and management has always been a family quarrel. They developed together, were interdependent, and expressed different aspects of the same institution. The trade-union was the inevitable grouping of the workers in modern industry. It expressed the laborer's part in the going concern. The destiny of the factory system was his destiny as well. In spite of the constant bickering and seeming civil war, the thing fought over was a common possession of the workers and the employers. From the beginning, the basic industrial discipline has identified the workers with each other in an organic group, and, as a group, with their job and their factory. Otherwise the persistent dissidence of a century and a half has been played out in a vacuum, which is nonsense.

The workers and their employers were caught up in the same going concern. Each trade-union contract accepted by management affected both the industry and the workers, and the results were not merely economic, but political, social, moral, and psychological as well. The participants in each collective bargain were never the same again, and therefore the society itself would never be the same again. All of the future would now be built upon the newer structure that the contract represented. But to the revolutionaries every bargain was a betrayal of their hope of cataclysm. Instead of accepting discord and strife between unions and management as indicative of a natural movement for remedial adjustment, and therefore a healthy thing, they chose to escape from the requisite conflicts by abolishing the society in which they arose. The revolutionaries believed that if they could be freed from these particular irritations they would escape from all of them. They chose to escape from the real world.

The revolutionary sects differed among themselves on how to reconvert the social order, but they all agreed that the great aim was a world in which irritations and dissidence would no longer arise. In this effort the intellectual redefined human nature as well as the social institutions in which man has his being. The ideas of the Utopians, whether classical economists, Socialists, Syndicalists, Communists, or anarchists, were equally antagonistic to the older notions of a cohesive society and of the place of man within it. The economist's ideal of perfect competition is in its way just as much a revolution as the classless society of the Communist. Both are a perversion of human nature and a denial of life because they both deny that man is a member of a society.

Therein lies the great gap between trade-unionism and Utopian or "scientific" socialism. The trade-unionist lived by the older values, derived from membership in a society. He fought his battles in the name of the older concepts of justice and freedom. But to the revolutionaries the effort to retrieve the old or reform the new was obstructionist. The acceptance of the world here and now by the trade-unions they found especially galling. To them the trade-union leader was a "petty bourgeois," a "misleader," and a "traitor." [3] The trade-union stood in the path and blocked the way to heaven upon earth.

The Socialists and the Communists have always considered themselves superior to the trade-unionists, and their parties were conceived as standing outside and as acting upon the trade-unions from above. They were to lead and inspire the workers' movement and to endow the amorphous mass with a consciousness and a will to forge the revolutionaries' dream. They were so sure of their ends, so certain of the inevitability of their objectives, that the labor leader who opposed their meddling was condemned as an enemy of the working class. A self-

[3] The old argument still continues: "One of the most vexatious and aggravating things . . . is that we in the labor unions who take the first bitter barrages of the Communist billingsgate—we who are labeled by the Communists, 'reactionaries,' 'red baiters,' 'shopowners stooges,' 'phonies,' 'labor fakirs,' 'misleaders of labor,' 'sell-out artists,' 'benevolent dictators,' 'two-faced schemers,' and a myriad of other lush lying propaganda words—we who are called 'war-mongering murderers' when we support the policy of this Government to keep our country strong—too often we are bombarded from the rear by what we should regard as our own heavy artillery." From *Hearings before the Joint Committee on Labor-Management Relations* (hereafter referred to as *Hearings, II*). Congress of the United States, 80th Congress, 2nd session, on the Operation of the Labor-Management Relations Act, 1947, p. 235, "Statement of Vincent J. Malone, President, Pacific Coast Firemen, Oilers, Watertenders and Wipers Association."

invoked hypnotism blinded the revolutionaries with the illusion that they were the only spokesmen of the working class. They had, in fact, taken over the role of the ancient Messiah, to lead the people out of the valley and unto the high mountains, to show them, not the next world, but the glory of this one, even if the people did not want to see it. That was, after all, a minor matter. The people would be persuaded and inspired, and they would see the light even against their will. "In what consists the role of the social-democracy," Lenin asked, "if not in being the 'spirit' . . . raising the elemental movement up to its program?" [4]

The Communists will raise up the working class by creating a party of iron. "The force of habit of millions and tens of millions is a most formidable force. Without a party of iron . . . it is impossible . . . to succeed." [5] In Russia, therefore, which is the model of all revolutionary movements and Communist Party objectives, "Not one important political or organizational question is decided by any state institution in our republic without the governing instruction of the central committee of the party." [6]

The trade-unions have to be captured because "the general tendency of capitalist production is not to raise but to sink the average standard of wages." [7] Trade-

[4] Quoted in Max Eastman: *Marxism, Is It Science?* (New York, 1940), p. 243.

[5] Ibid., p. 236.

[6] Quoted from Lenin, ibid., p. 232.

[7] Karl Marx: "Value, Price and Profit," in *Selected Works* (New York: International Publishers; 1939), Vol. I, p. 337.

The record, of course, is quite different. "What has actually hap-

unions are a misguided and wasted effort because "they are fighting with the effects but not with the cause of those effects. . . . They are applying palliatives, not curing the malady." [8] Trade-unions must aim at the larger goal. "They ought therefore not to be exclusively absorbed in these unavoidable guerilla fights . . . [but] inscribe on their banner the revolutionary watchword: *Abolition of the wage system.*" [9] This theme runs through Marx's writing whenever he touches on the trade-union.

In the decisions of the International Workingmen's Association we find the same idea. "The trade unions must now learn how to act consciously as focal points for organizing the working class in the greater interest of its complete emancipation." The great aim of labor organizations must be the final revolution, because, "the working class is revolutionary or it is nothing." [10]

Friedrich Engels shares Marx's view. The trade-unions are not sufficient for the purpose of the revolution. "Something more is needed than trade unions and strikes to break the power of the ruling class." [11] In 1879 Engels criticized the English trade-union movement because it

pened is that hourly money wages have risen perhaps eightfold from 1820 to 1938, and hourly real wages fivefold in the same period, though prices showed no strong and consistent trend in either direction, except for the effect of the first World War. From 1820 to 1945 the rise is about thirteenfold in hourly money wages and sixfold in real wages." John Maurice Clark: *Alternative to Serfdom* (New York: Alfred A. Knopf; 1948), p. 131.

[8] Marx, op. cit., p. 337.

[9] Ibid.

[10] Karl Marx and Friedrich Engels: *Selected Correspondence* (New York: International Publishers; 1942), p. 189.

[11] Quoted in A. Lozovsky: *Marx and the Trade Unions* (New York: International Publishers; 1942), p. 49.

had devoted its energies to the "strike for wages and shorter working hours . . . as an end in itself." [12] The remedy for this preoccupation with the practical and the immediate was to "work inside of them, to form within this still quite plastic mass a core of people . . . who will take over the leadership . . . when the . . . impending breakup of the present 'order' takes place." [13] This was Engels's prescription for the Knights of Labor, and the idea of "boring from within" and capturing the leadership has been applied by the Socialists and Communists wherever they could. They are still doing it. The trade-union is important only if it can be taken over by the elect and used for preconceived ends. They are the people "whose minds are theoretically clear," and who can explain and hammer home the point that every movement is bound to fail and go astray unless it keeps continually before itself "the destruction of the wage system." [14] It is therefore the duty of those possessed of the true faith to see to it that the unions are "revolutionized from within." [15]

These ideas were taken over by Lenin and elaborated into a working technique. Lenin documents his own working philosophy of the danger of trade-unions becoming bourgeois-minded, and hence an impediment to the revolution, by citing Marx and Engels to establish the legitimacy of his position.[16]

[12] Karl Marx and Friedrich Engels, op. cit., pp. 420–1.
[13] Ibid., pp. 450–1.
[14] Ibid., p. 452.
[15] Ibid., p. 453.
[16] "Here (in reference to a statement in *The Poverty of Philosophy*, Charles H. Kerr & Co., 1910, p. 188) we have the programme and the

With so much support from the major prophets, Lenin voiced his conviction with an unquestioning self-assurance. In 1900 he said: "Isolated from Social-Democracy, the labour movement becomes petty and inevitably becomes bourgeois: in conducting only the economic struggle, the working class loses its political independence; it becomes the tail of the other parties and runs counter to the great slogan: 'The emancipation of the workers must be the task of the workers themselves.'" [17]

It is just this, of course, that the revolutionaries must prevent. The workers must by all means be kept from

tactics of the economic struggle and the trade union movement for several decades to come, for the whole long period in which the workers are preparing for 'a future battle.' We must place side by side with this a number of references by Marx and Engels to the example of the British labour movement; how in consequence of industrial 'prosperity,' attempts are made 'to buy the workers' (*Briefwechsel*, Vol. I, p. 136), to distract them from the struggle; how, generally speaking, this prosperity 'demoralizes the workers' (Vol. II, p. 218); how the British proletariat is becoming 'bourgeoisified'; how 'the ultimate aim of this most bourgeois of all nations seems to be to establish a bourgeois aristocracy and a bourgeois proletariat side by side with the bourgeoisie' (Vol. II, p. 290); how the 'revolutionary energy' of the British proletariat oozes away (Vol. III, p. 124); how it will be necessary to wait for a considerable time 'before the British workers can rid themselves of their apparent bourgeois corruption' (Vol. III, p. 127); how the British movement 'lacks the mettle of the Chartists' (1866: Vol. III, p. 305); how the British workers' leaders are developing into something between 'a radical bourgeois and a worker' (Vol. IV, p. 209, on Holyoake); how owing to British monopoly, and as long as that monopoly lasts 'the British workingman will not budge' (Vol. IV, p. 433). The tactics of the economic struggle, in connection with the general course (and *the outcome*) of the labour movement, are here considered from a remarkably broad, many-sided, dialectical, and genuinely revolutionary outlook." V. I. Lenin: *Karl Marx*, in *Selected Works* (New York: International Publishers), Vol. I, p. 50.

[17] "The Struggle for the Bolshevik Party (1900–1904)," written in 1900, in V. I. Lenin: *Selected Works*, Vol. II, p. 11.

"lapsing from Social Democracy to trade unionism." Because trade-unions inevitably reveal "a certain tendency to be non-political," it is the broader duty of the party "to educate and guide the trade unions." [18] This education has but one purpose: to subject the trade-union movement to the control of the Communist Party. The Communist Party can achieve its ends only by capturing the trade-unions. It was accomplished in Russia, and if the Communists have their way, it will be done everywhere else.[19]

The Communists have followed their masters' inspiration to the logical conclusion: the capture, use, and emasculation of the trade-union movement. The workers' organizations could have no purpose that the Communists

[18] V. I. Lenin: *Left-Wing Communism, an Infantile Disorder* (New York: International Publishers; 1940), p. 34.

[19] How it worked out in Russia is stated by Lenin himself in very convincing terms. In *Left-Wing Communism, an Infantile Disorder*, Lenin was answering some of the German "Left" Communists and their hands-off policy toward "reactionary" trade-unions. At this point in the argument he describes the function of trade-unions, with particular reference to the Soviet Union:

"In its work the Party relies directly on the *trade unions*, which at present, according to the data of the last congress (April, 1920) have over 4,000,000 members, and which are formally *non-party*. Actually, all the directing bodies of the vast majority of the unions . . . consist of Communists and carry out all the instructions of the Party. Thus, on the whole, we have a formally non-Communist, flexible and relatively wide and very powerful proletarian apparatus, by means of which the Party is closely linked up with the *class* and with the *masses*, and by means of which, under the leadership of the Party, *the dictatorship of the class* is effected. Without close contact with the trade union, without their hearty support and self-sacrificing work, not only in economic *but also in military affairs*, it would, of course, have been impossible for us to govern the country and to maintain the dictatorship for two months, let alone two years." (Italics in the source quoted.) Lenin: *Left-Wing Communism*, ed. cit., p. 32.

needed to respect except that which fitted in with the political and revolutionary aims of the Communist Party. Apart from that, the trade-union movement was for the workers a sort of misguided effort that led them in a "bourgeois" direction. And that, of course, was both dangerous and obstructionist to the Communist plan to save the workers, even against their will.

This clear denial of the significance of trade-unionism, except as an instrument, holds true of all social-revolutionary movements. The Socialists, like the Communists, have a purpose beyond trade-unionism, and the trade-unions must be the tool for the fulfillment of future plans. According to Karl Kautsky, the trade-unions are important only as they lead to the social revolution. They are important "as militant organizations, not as organizations for social peace." This is due to the fact that up to the present they have proved "at most only a nuisance to the employers." [20]

The Socialists, no matter how conciliatory and conservative, found it impossible to escape their sense of superior mission and insight. Morris Hilquit declared modestly that "the only difference between the socialists and trade unionists . . . is that . . . the former clearly realize this ultimate goal [the end of capitalism] . . . the latter do not." [21] Daniel De Leon was more forthright in his assertion of the greater Socialist wisdom and insight. He saw that "a thing called a union may act as

[20] Karl Kautsky: *On the Morrow of the Social Revolution* (London: 20th Century Press; 1907), pp. 34–5.

[21] Morris Hilquit: *Socialism in Theory and Practice* (New York, 1909), p. 240.

a drag upon the Socialist movement." [22] The immediate demands may prove a trap unless they meet the test: "Does the contemplated step square with the ultimate aim?" Otherwise it is a "trap and disastrous." It is thus the bounden duty of those who see the ultimate aim to equip the trade-union movement with "the proper knowledge." [23]

As can be seen, the motive remains the same. The trade-unions are mere instruments to be molded, and their members indoctrinated, by those who know the truth and the way. The many years of bitter struggle between Daniel De Leon and Samuel Gompers were over just this issue. To Gompers, the trade-union movement was an institution in its own right; to De Leon, as to all other radicals, it was either a means to the larger end they had in view or it was nothing. If the trade-union movement did not go the way the Socialists wanted it to go, then it was a "trap."

Eugene Debs, when he became a convert to Socialism, took a similar view. The trade-union movement was to be imbued with the larger purpose. The labor movement means "infinitely more than a paltry increase in wages. . . . Its higher object is to overthrow the capitalist system. . . ." [24]

The Syndicalists, starting with the ideas of Marx,[25]

[22] Daniel De Leon: "The Burning Question of Trade Unionism," delivered in Newark, N.J., on April 21, 1904 (New York: Labor News Co.), p. 31.

[23] Ibid., pp. 34–6.

[24] Eugene V. Debs: *Writings and Speeches* (New York: Heritage Press; 1948), pp. 107–8. Written in 1904.

[25] "Marx supposes, exactly as the Syndicalists do, that the revolu-

had their own role for the trade-unions. They, too, would guide them in the direction in which they ought to go. The decentralized trade-unions would inherit the powers of the state without inheriting its evils. The General Strike, which would usher in the future, would not merely destroy the capitalist system, but would also endow the workers with a mystical sense of duty, purity, and virtue that would shine forever. Heaven would come by a cataclysm and remain unblemished for all time.

The trade-union, as a going concern enmeshed in the complexities of an industrial society, striving to adjust to the shifting pressures of daily life, and the ever changing needs of men and communities, was not acceptable even among the Syndicalists. To them the trade-union was useful only for what it will do in the future. Its present role is to prepare for the day after the cataclysm.

Caught up as they were in the same body of theory, the anarchists, as represented by Bakunin, had very much the same reaction to the trade-unions as the Socialists, Communists, and Syndicalists. The workers and their organizations are to be molded and directed. The strike is important because it "is the beginning of the social war between the proletariat and the bourgeoisie" and deepens the antagonism between the classes in society. "The strike is a war, and the masses organize only during time of war." It is then that "the indignant masses are as molten metal, which poured and fused into one solid mass, can be formed more easily than cold metal, provided good

---

tion will be absolute and irrevocable." George Sorel: *Reflections on Violence* (New York, 1941), p. 183.

masters are found." And who could be better masters than the anarchists? The objective is the same as with all of the other revolutionaries: to prepare the workers and their unions for "that terrible social revolution which we now foresee." [26] The cataclysm is the important thing. The rest will take care of itself. Like the Syndicalists, Bakunin has great faith in the future. It is only the present he would destroy, and his instrument, his only instrument, is the trade-union.

The position of the revolutionaries with respect to the trade union movement remains substantially the same, regardless of the ideological differences among them. For all of them, it could be said by changing the word "Communist" to "Socialist," "Syndicalist," or even "Anarchist," that: "It is the bounden duty of every Communist to belong to a trade union, even a most reactionary one, provided it is a mass organization. Only by constant and persistent work in the trade unions and in the factories for the steadfast and energetic defence of the interests of the workers, together with ruthless struggle against the reformist bureaucracy, will it be possible to win the leadership in the workers' struggle and to win the industrially organised workers over to the side of the Party." [27]

In short, the "idealists" of whatever category proved psychologically incapable of recognizing the trade-union

[26] Mikhail Bakunin, quoted in A. Lozovsky: *Marx and the Trade Unions*, pp. 131–2.

[27] From *The Programme of the Communist International*, adopted at the Sixth Congress of the Communist International in 1928. In *A Handbook of Marxism*, edited by Emile Burns (New York: Random House; 1935), pp. 1038–9.

movement as important in itself. They insisted on meddling in the trade-union movement to promote ends peculiar to their own view of the nature of society and the purpose of man. None of them accepted trade-unionism as sufficient for the purpose for which it was organized. The specific reasons for which the workers organized seemed unimportant, incidental, or even detrimental. If the workers devoted themselves to improving wages, bettering conditions of labor, shortening hours, and acquiring status within the industry, they would become "business-minded" and prove less tractable to the hand of the revolutionary.

None of the revolutionaries are prepared to live in this world here and now. They must always have their eyes upon the great beyond, after they have destroyed the present world by precipitating a cataclysm. Millennialism is the ever present reality. The revolutionists will have only what they cannot achieve—the peace that knows no alteration, no movement, no friction, and no life. The revolutionaries never understood, and do not understand now, that the organization of a trade-union makes the total society in which that union operates different. The union is not an instrument against society; it is an additional way of organizing society, not merely its labor, but in all of its other forms.

When a trade-union movement comes into being, the politics, the economy, the family, the morals, the status of men among men, the motivations and the ends, the very means of survival, are modified. The trade-union, just because it is immersed in details, is in some degree the society itself. Organized labor is not merely an economic, or political, or social movement. It is all of these and more; it is the whole society cast in an additional pattern.

It was, however, the trade-union's immersion in the details and compromises of daily living that made it seem unimportant to the revolutionary. The revolutionary is concerned with the broad plan, the establishment of "a classless society," an "anarcho-communist society," or "the dictatorship of the proletariat." It is natural that the commitment to a universal design should make him contemptuous of trade-unionism as something of no major significance unless he could bend it to his own broad ends. He could not accept the trade-union, because that would have involved the recognition of the complexity of the social structure and would automatically have defeated every attempt to pattern the world according to his heart's desire.

The trade-union movement, therefore, has had few friends. Everyone seemed to know where the trade-union ought to go except the trade-unionist. The trade-unionist himself has been inarticulate. His strength lay in the fact that one thing he could not yield: his immediate ends, the only ones of which he was conscious. If he did, he would deny his own career. Like a true churchman of any denomination, or like a good businessman, he could not agree that the charges made from the outside were true, or that the outsider really understood him, or that anyone but the trade-union movement itself could attempt to remedy its faults. He had to live by the light that was in him and to resist attempts by outsiders either to disrupt or to capture his organization.

To Marx, Engels, Kautsky, Hilquit, De Leon, Sorel, Lenin, Bakunin, and others, *the revolution* was the one great end to which all must be subordinated. To them, the interests of the workers in the immediate, the particular, the local, the tangible things—shorter hours, better wages, greater freedom within the industry—were delusive. These "economic exposures" were only a phase of "bourgeois politics." The business of the intellectual leader, the idealist, was "to march ahead of the spontaneous movement," because to the intellectual the end is more important than the means, whereas to the trade-union the daily compromise with the details of a complex industrial world is the substance of its existence and survival.

The argument over the trade-unions has now lasted something like a hundred and fifty years and is still going on. The economists' reconciliation to the workers' organizations has been slow and only half-hearted. Few professional economists are willing to accept trade-unionism on economic grounds as a positive agency in increased production and a force in raising the standard of living of the mass of the people. It has not proved easy to move from the belief that workers' organizations are a hindrance and a disturbance to the idea that they are a beneficent and constructive force in the economic process. At best, they are credited with (1) protecting the workers against exploitation; (2) contributing to the development of mass production by increasing the purchasing power of the workers; (3) forcing greater efficiency upon industry to meet the challenge of higher costs.

Those economists have proved most friendly who recognize trade-unionism as useful on social and political grounds. The economists are trying to preserve their theoretical "model" of free enterprise, and are adapting themselves to the idea of a competitive economy based upon large groups rather than upon individuals.[28]

[28] The following citations illustrate the varying attitudes of economists who have had to face the trade-union as a going concern.

1. "If he is banded with his fellows, if he possesses the wherewithal to make a trial of strength, and if he has shrewd and well-informed leaders he bargains to the best advantage." F. W. Taussig: *Wages and Capital* (New York: D. Appleton & Co.; 1896), p. 79.

2. "Whether the organization of labour has created the conditions assuring a rise in wages, or better earnings through more continuous employment, when those conditions would not have been established through the changes in the general economic situation, is an unanswered question." A. W. Flux: *Economic Principles* (London, Methuen & Co.; 1904), pp. 141–2.

3. "Wages, we say, are measured by the marginal productivity of labor. This productivity, in turn, is partially dependent upon the demand and supply of labor. But the supply of labor is largely controlled, as we have seen, by the standard of life; and one of the great functions of the labor organizations is to strengthen and advance the standard of life." R. T. Ely: *Outlines of Economics* (New York: Macmillan Co.; 1914), p. 389.

4. "The theory of wages that has been explained in these pages is that under conditions of free, all-sided competition workmen will tend to secure wages corresponding closely to the additions their labor makes to the value of the product. . . . The very best they can do for their members is to secure for them the full competitive rate." H. R. Seager: *Principles of Economics* (New York: Henry Holt & Co.; 1913), pp. 554–5.

5. "The policy of standardised conditions also has a favorable effect for entrepreneurs, in so far as it drives out of business those undertakings which are unable to pay standard wages or generally to maintain the standard conditions. . . . The necessity for observing the standard conditions compels the adoption of the best possible organisation and

In the meantime the effort of the Communists to secure control of the labor unions has become increasingly acrimonious and vituperative, for with the growth of the power of organized labor the stakes are larger, and the

---

the greatest technical perfection in industry." G. Cassel: *The Theory of Social Economy* (New York: Harcourt, Brace & Co.; 1932), p. 318.

6. "Hence, a member of a strong union can go ahead in production with somewhat less fear that the rate will be arbitrarily cut if he makes good wages. . . . Restrictions of output must be balanced, therefore, against compensating gains in production derived from the protection which the union affords the worker." W. E. Atkins et al.: *Economic Behavior* (Boston: Houghton Mifflin Co.; 1931), Vol. II, p. 200.

7. "The pressure for high wages exerted by the trade-union is a constant goad to managerial efficiency. The employer is forced to buckle down to the job of making industry efficient enough to carry the load of high wages." F. B. Garver and A. H. Hansen: *Principles of Economics* (Boston: Ginn & Co.; 1937), pp. 482–3.

8. ". . . the benefits conferred by any particular trade-union cease with the prevention of exploitation. The fixing of a wage, by a trade union, which is above the marginal product of the existing number of workers in the trade will force the employers to contract output and discharge laborers until a higher price for the product is reached at which wages and marginal products are again equal. The laborers who are thrown out of work because of the higher wage will have to seek employment in other trades, and their addition to the supply will tend to depress wages in those other trades. At the same time, all other workers will have to pay a higher price for fewer goods made by the high-wage trade-union labor." A. L. Meyers: *Elements of Modern Economics* (New York: Prentice-Hall; 1938) p. 197.

9. "But a high price is paid for these gains; the area of competition and freedom of enterprise is much restricted. Men who cannot earn the standard rate must remain unemployed or force wage rates still lower in the shrinking number of unorganized industries." R. T. Bye and W. W. Hewett: *Applied Economics* (New York, F. S. Crofts & Co.; 1947), p. 171.

10. "There can, humanly speaking, be no doubt that real wages in this country would have risen spectacularly with or without unions; and perhaps nearly as much as they have actually risen. . . . But without unions, human rights on the job would have made for slower progress." J. M. Clark: *Guidepost to Social Change* (1949) p. 148.

hope of revolution, if the control of the trade-union movement could be secured, more imminent. The Communists have not, however, secured complete control over the trade-union movements except in countries where they previously had achieved political control. Even in such countries as France and Italy, where the labor movement has long been subjected to political manipulation, the Communists, in spite of every effort, have fallen short of their objectives. Other claimants have disputed the Communists' pretensions to represent the workers—the Socialists, the Syndicalists, and the Catholic unions. There has also been a substratum of "pure and simple" trade-unionism that has stood its ground against all the blandishments of political sirens.

It is not an accident that in the most fully developed industrial countries, Great Britain and the United States, control over the trade-unions by political parties has been least effective. That is true in Great Britain even today, where the Labour Party is in power, for here the trade-unions may be said to control the Labour Party. The Labour Party has won over the trade-union leaders to its own program, but it does not run the trade-unions, and it lives upon the sufferance of organized labor.

The record shows that the intellectual reformers and revolutionaries who were most vociferous in their criticism of the evils of our developing industrial society were least aware of the meaning of the humble trade-unions established by the workers in their own defense. They failed to see that the labor unions were an organic growth in modern society, and that they fulfilled a necessary and inevitable service in re-creating a "society" within which the worker could regain his dignity as a man and once again play the part of a moral person.

CHAPTER VII

Owner and Laborer

IF THE "society" represented by trade-unionism has returned to the worker a sense of identity within a moral universe, it has also raised unforeseen difficulties. The character of trade-unionism has been deeply affected by the changes that have occurred within our modern economy. In theory, labor was treated as impersonal, pecuniary, and fluid. A man was (and still is) hired for the job by the day, or even by the hour. Not only is he free to leave his job, but the doctrine of competition made it advisable for him to do so if a better job was available. He had no responsibility to the employer, to the enterprise, to the body politic—only to himself. His advantage was measured by pecuniary returns—that is, the price of labor. Thus theory fitted a substantial body of actual experience. The migration of labor from rural to urban communities, and from one country to another as well, the labor turnover, the repeated sampling of different jobs by workers in their search for a better niche, the ebb and flow of employment with the economic cycle, the periodic change of occupation in seasonal industries, the shifts in employment resulting from new machines, all induced a feeling of insecurity, a habit of wandering, and an essential indifference to any given job.

The identity of this instability with an ever varying wage gave the entire process a singularly amoral implication. This does not deny that there were innumerable cases of continuity in a given job, business, or skill. But the over-all feeling was one of insecurity. Anyone who has seen workers lined up for a job in front of a factory gate during periods of unemployment, or wandering from one establishment to another, or answering an advertisement for "hands" and finding hundreds of others there ahead of him, will recognize the psychological and moral implications of this separation between the human being and the thing worked at, or the shop worked in.

The sense of identity between the worker and his job had been broken, but so had the relationship between the owner and the thing he owned. The industrial structure had been altered. The millions of owners of stock (and sometimes the hundreds of thousands in a single large corporation) have ownership without knowledge, without direct responsibility, and without moral commitment. If they are dissatisfied, they sell their holdings and buy into another enterprise. They are like the worker who seeks a better job, who gets tired of working in one place, who stands in line waiting for employment, or who scans the help-wanted advertisements to see if a good opportunity is opening in some other place. We thus have a double fluidity, both of labor and of ownership, and a double irresponsibility. In each case the controlling motive is pecuniary. Large numbers of both workers and owners are now in the same boat: they make their living from an enterprise to which they have no moral commitment and in which they merely seek an opportunity for pecuniary gain.

The days of proprietary ownership by the individual, the family, or the partnership, where the living to be gained was dependent upon constant attention to details and the exercise of personal responsibility, has increasingly given way to a fluid, impersonal relation to the industries from which people draw their livings. The novelty of the corporation is not merely its size or great wealth, but what it has done to ownership. Under corporate form, the purchaser of stock has an ownership of which he can divest himself at a moment's notice. His relationship is pecuniary, and he measures the prospect of profit in ways that bedevil the subtlest of psychologists or economists. He and the other stockholders own the industry, but they are not acquainted with the managers; they do not even know the names of the board of directors. They make no administrative decisions affecting the enterprise; they feel no direct responsibility for its operations, and would be incapable of expressing a sound judgment upon its multitudinous problems if called upon to do so. The industry is operated by the management in the name of the owners, the management itself owning little or no stock in the industry. While the management is responsible to the owners, whom it does not know, in practice it reports to the directors, who again may or may not be owners, and may or may not be skilled in the problems of the industry. The board of directors is often selected by the management for election by the stockholders. The chief duty of the directors is to approve the policies proposed by the management. The board of directors acts in the name of the stockholders, and secures an annual vote of confidence from the "owners" if it can gather a sufficient number of proxies. That is not always easy, not because the stockholders refuse to approve the policy of the managers, but because they are often so indifferent to the issue raised that they do not even return the solicited proxy.

In addition, the stock purchased by the investor is not representative of any specific piece of tangible real property. What the purchaser secures is a bundle of rights. But the bundle of rights is variable in form and content because the contractual arrangement which the stock-purchaser accepts differs from company to company, and may differ from stock issue to stock issue in the same company. When the purchaser is not fully aware (and he rarely is) of the specific limitation and rights of the particular share of stock he buys, his purchase may be a blind response to an optimistic hope of a good return, based upon a rumor, an inside tip, a hunch, or poor resistance to a good sales talk. What he really buys is a bundle of rights in the good judgment, integrity, and competence of a board of directors whom he does not know. It would be better to say that what a man purchases in the stock market is an expectancy of an income. He does not buy a business, and assumes no responsibility for earning the income. In fact, the income, even if earned, may in part or in totality be kept from him at the discretion of the board of directors and put to other purposes, such as expansion, amortization, reserves, or other legitimate ends deemed necessary by the managers of the corporation. What has happened is that the property of yesterday has become an indefinite claim against a corporation managed by people who do not own it. What the stockholder owns he measures "in a market quotation." [1]

This anomalous and unlooked-for outcome, in which neither owner nor laborer has any moral identification with his source of livelihood, is not durable. It is not given that a society shall continue which requires that the mass of the folk who make their living through ownership or labor shall have no concern with the source of their livelihood. The difficulty is upon us, even if its recognition has lagged behind the facts. It is a changing situation in which many vestiges of the older structure persist, and where the older philosophy has contributed a covering mantle for an unexpected development.

In its essence, trade-unionism is a revulsion against social atomization on the one hand, and the divorce of owner and worker from their historical function as moral agents in industry on the other. If there is any meaning that can be derived from the persistent grouping of men about their tools or within their industry, it is that work

[1] A. A. Berle and G. C. Means: *The Modern Corporation and Private Property* (New York: Macmillan Co.; 1931), pp. 277–8.

must fill a social and moral as well as an economic role. The vacuum created between the job and the man has proved intolerable; and it cannot be filled by higher wages, shorter hours, better conditions of labor, music in the shops, or baby clinics. Man has to belong to something real, purposeful, useful, creative; he must belong to his job and to his industry, or it must belong to him. There is no way of permanently separating the two. What gnaws at the psychological and moral roots of the contemporary world is that most urban people, workers and owners, belong to nothing real, nothing greater than their own impersonal pecuniary interests. To escape from this profound tragedy of our industrial society is the great issue of our time, for a world in which neither the owner nor the worker is morally identified with his source of income has no principle of continuity. No institution can survive for long in a moral vacuum. For the worker the trade-union has represented an unwitting attempt to escape from this dilemma.

There is a continuing failure to recognize that the trade-union, like the corporation, represents a structural change within the economy. The trade-union is not a reform movement; it is not a political party; it is not revolutionary in intent; it is not a legislative activity. It may at times contribute to all of these, but it is none of them. It is the formal expression of the socially inevitable grouping of men in modern industry, just as the corporation and the holding company are new ways of organizing capital for industry. The trade-union is the opposite side of the metal. Where you have corporate industry, there you have the modern national labor union. As long as industry and commerce were small and proprietary the very nature of the trade-union was different.

A persistent tendency toward monopoly is the logical consequence of a free market, in either industry or labor. There are many areas where monopoly is incomplete, or only incipient. There are few areas in our economy where the effort to escape the insecurities of the competitive market has not set in motion tendencies which, if unchecked, or perhaps even in spite of legal prohibition, may achieve monopolistic results. The older society of individual ownership of property on the one hand, and of stable, conscientious labor on the other, has been transmuted into something very different. Ownership and labor have become, as we have seen, fluid, impersonal, and frequently temporary relationships to a source of income. The present job, like the share of stock, is subject to change without notice. The income that both are expected to provide may decline or disappear because no other job is to be had or because the prospective yield on the stock did not materialize. In either case the worker and the stockholder are helpless. The worker must await the day when employment opportunities have improved and more jobs are available, and the stockholder must pray for a turn in the "business tide," and for a profitable "quarter," so that the board of directors will feel free to declare a substantial dividend.

The striking feature of this situation is that both worker and stockholder are individually helpless. The small stockholder—and he is now numbered in the millions—

can do nothing to recover his money or to secure the expected income. He has no powers or instrumentalities that are immediately effective. Stockholders' committees are notoriously a dubious recourse, and action in court is expensive, time-consuming, and unpredictable. Of course, the stockholder may have no legitimate complaint. If there is a serious recession in business, the board of directors, with the best management in the world, has no choice but to pass over a dividend on the stock. As a last resort the stockholder can sell his shares, but if business is bad the value of the stock will have declined far below what he paid for it and far below its potential value.

If the owner of this new fluid and "immaterial" property is helpless, so too is the worker. The plant closes down, and he loses his job for no reason that he can understand. All he knows is that a notice appeared on the wall to the effect that after the close of the week the factory would remain shut indefinitely. There may be no other plant in town, or no other job even if there are other factories. The worker can do nothing; he has no one to blame; no one may be at fault. His savings, if any, will soon be gone. What next? Like the stockholder, he is one of many who are in the same position, all of them helpless in a crisis that affects their very means of subsistence, their place in the community, their position as effective citizens of a town or city. In an extreme case they are both forced upon public charity.

An interesting aspect of this strange relationship of the individual to the economy is its anonymous character.

The worker and the stockholder are both anonymous, both subject to forces over which they have no control, both made to accept a decision from people whom they do not know. Their fortunes are decided for them without reference to their individual needs or peculiar state of dependence upon either the job or the yield from stock-ownership. Such a state of fluidity and anonymity has never before been characteristic of so large a part of the total population as it is at present. It is not, and may not become, universal, but the fear of individual insecurity and the feeling of helplessness have cut deeply into the consciousness of our times. It is here that the developing industrialism has done its greatest harm to the individual. The many goods and services, the freedoms and opportunities, that have come to us through thousands of inventions are excellent things, but the price has been high.

It is a curious fact that individual isolation and fluidity should have gone hand in hand with the concentration of power in corporations, holding companies, and cartels. We have an increasing individual helplessness of both owner and laborer, accompanied by an increasing size, power, and dominance of the corporation that provides the work and earns the income. No such picture of the economic institution could have been drawn in the past. In a measure, the corporations, the owner, and the worker are all anonymous, except that the corporation has a life and resiliency that are independent of the worker and, to an increasing extent, of the owner. If sufficent reserves could be set aside for new capital outlay, the corporation could, in theory at least, temporarily become completely independent of its nominal owners.

The corporation has grown in size and influence since the Civil War. Changes in corporation law since then, permitting corporations to own stocks of other corporations, have made possible the pyramiding of ownership and power in anonymous bodies that stand like great giants in a world of personally helpless men and women, whether they are workers or owners. How great the concentration of power has become was recently (1939–40) illumined by the Temporary National Economic Committee of the United States Congress.

Before the war there were thirty corporations in the United States with assets of more than a billion dollars each. These giant economic units are each richer than many an American state or sovereign foreign nation. Only ten states have "within their border property and wealth" of greater value than the largest corporation in the United States.[2] The two largest corporations, the Metropolitan Life Insurance Company and the American Telephone and Telegraph Company, are wealthier than any one of thirty-eight states in the United States. To describe the issue more graphically: the Pennsylvania Railroad is richer than the state of Kansas; the Chase National Bank than the state of Minnesota; the United States Steel Corporation than West Virginia; General Motors than Tennessee; Cities Service Company than the state of Colorado; North American Company than South Dakota or Florida. In fact, each of eighteen states are

[2] David Lynch: *The Concentration of Economic Power* (New York: Columbia University Press; 1947), p. 113.

poorer than any one of the smallest of the thirty billion-dollar corporations existing before the war.

The corporations control 100 per cent of the production of gas and electric power, 96 per cent of mining, 92 per cent of manufacturing, 89 per cent of transportation, and 84 per cent of finance. How concentrated the economy has become is evidenced by the fact that 1 per cent of the employers in the United States hire 48 per cent of the workers, and that 5 per cent give employment to 70 per cent of those working for wages.

While there were some 400,000 corporations in the United States in 1940, less than 1 per cent of these held 52 per cent of all the corporate assets. This concentration of wealth is reflected in production: one company produces 100 per cent of the aluminum; three companies, 86 per cent of the automobiles; three companies, 90 per cent of tin cans; three companies, 80 per cent of cigarettes; four companies, 100 per cent of corn binders; two companies, 95 per cent of plate glass; two companies, 90 per cent of safety glass.

The point is clear: in size, labor employed, and production the larger corporations dominate certain large areas of American economic life. In the glass industry, for instance, the parent company, through the control of patents, regulates production and allocates markets, decides who can or cannot go into the glass-producing business, determines the type of bottle or glass that can be produced and the quantity that can be placed on the market, and fixes the prices. Independent producers find the going hard, and by a series of litigations for patent infringement, the smaller independent companies were either forced into bankruptcy or compelled to sell out or join the larger company.

There are, of course, advantages that can be ascribed to concentration: more research, improved products, lower prices, wider distribution of the best standard product, and increased convenience and higher standards of living for the mass of the people. All of this certainly has truth, but it is also true that it has been paralleled by an increasing divorce on the part of both the stock-owner and the worker from moral responsibility for the process of production.

The American Telephone and Telegraph Company owns 93 per cent of the voting stock in twenty-one associated companies, whose operations cover all of the United States. Directly or through subsidiaries it controls over 50 per cent of the voting stock in 181 corporations, with assets of some five billion dollars. The telephone companies controlled by these corporations employ 300,000 workers, and the ownership is in the hands of 700,000 stockholders. The corporation serves 15,000,000 customers, and has a gross revenue of over a billion dollars a year. It controls from its central office in New York some 90 per cent of the local telephone service over the entire nation, 98 per cent of the long-distance telephone wires, and 100 per cent of the wire used in transmission of radio programs, as well as 100 per cent of teletype and transoceanic radio telephone service. It owned the Western Electric Company, which until recently made the greater part of all the telephone equipment used in the

United States. The president of the company can vote its stock in the operating companies and thus select the officers and directors of these concerns. The American telephone system, with all its complicated connections, is controlled by this one corporation. If this is an unusual example in magnitude and wealth, it is nevertheless illustrative of a drift in the American economy.[3]

This tendency has continued since the war. Since 1940 some 1,800 independent firms, with assets of over four billion dollars, have been bought by, or merged with, larger corporations. The great corporations came out of the war with such large amounts of liquid capital that they could have purchased a very large proportion of the smaller manufacturing corporations in the United States.[4]

It is clear that we have been moving at an accelerating pace from individual to corporate ownership. If it can be said that "management" is responsible to the stockholder (the nominal owner) and protects his interests, then the national trade union can be said to protect the interests of the worker. The corporation has given the national union its present significance. It may not have given it its birth, but today the United States Steel Corporation and the United States Steel Workers Union are counterparts of the industry. The growing monopoly of capital is faced by the growing monopoly of labor.

[3] Most of the material on corporations is drawn from the Temporary National Economic Committee's *Hearings and Reports,* as summarized by David Lynch, op. cit., Chapter vi.

[4] Federal Trade Commission: *Report on Present Trend of Corporate Mergers and Acquisitions* (Washington, D.C.: Government Printing Office; 1947) pp. 6–9.

CHAPTER VIII

Monopoly

THE MOVEMENT toward monopoly in industry has its parallel in the trade-unions. Trade-unionism is restrictive, arbitrary, often at war within itself, costly, and in contradiction to all the theories of a free market. So, too, is the corporation. If ownership is going to be divorced from direct responsibility, be impersonal, pecuniary, and fluid and increasingly represented by powerful corporations, labor, which is also fluid, impersonal, pecuniary, and without responsibility, is going to be organized into powerful unions. Paralleling the organization of corporate industry, the union does for the worker what the corporation does for the owner. If "management" represents the owner—that is, the fluid stockholder—and attempts to protect his pecuniary interests, then the labor leader represents the worker and attempts to protect his pecuniary interests.

There is one great difference, however, between the role of the "fluid" owner and the worker in modern industry. The worker, but not the owner, still has to be physically present in the factory or on the job. This need for physical participation is one of the important differences between the owner and the laborer and has conditioned the activities of the union. It is the presence of the worker in the shop that explains a major part of the trade-union's activities. For the worker, pecuniary stability depends upon the security of the job. To make the job secure and, secondly, to force it to yield a high monetary reward have been the lasting aims of trade-union policy. That these ends may be incompatible, that a high wage and job security may in any given case prove destructive of each other, is a bit of economic wisdom that is hard to learn, not only for the workers but also for the owners, who on more than one occasion have sacrificed their long-run interests to the irresistible lure of an immediate high gain.

The need for economic security is implicit in almost every trade-union demand. The current insistence upon health, old-age, and unemployment benefits to be derived from a tax on production, as in coal, or by contract, as in steel, is merely a newer phase of an older drive. Nor can these new goals be separated from continuing pressure for the closed shop, the check-off, seniority, and the hundred other items each of which is viewed as one more brick in the wall against insecurity. In making the union his chief instrument for the achievement of these ends, the worker has created an institution of great power and expanding influence. From the small beginnings of a local union there followed, as a matter of inner logic and necessity, the growth of other similar locals, and these in turn federated into national or international organizations embracing all the plants in an industry. The drive in each instance may be local and individual, but the sum of these local movements is a drift of vast proportions, changing the relationship of man to his work and of men to one another.

The present membership of trade-unions in the United States is around fifteen million, grouped in 197 national and international organizations, most of which are federated either in the American Federation of Labor or in the Council of Industrial Organizations, while 55 unions are independent. These organizations vary greatly in size. There are a few unions, such as the United Automobile Workers, the United Steel Workers of America, and the International Brotherhood of Teamsters, that claim approximately a million members each, but most labor organizations have fewer than 100,000 members.[1] In 1948 unionism was sufficiently inclusive so that roughly "one out of every six persons aged 21 years or over [was] a member of a labor organization." [2]

Equally revealing is the fact that organized labor represents between eighty and one hundred per cent of the employees engaged in producing agricultural equipment, aircraft and parts, aluminum, automobiles and parts, breweries, carpets and rugs, cement, clocks and watches, men's clothing, women's clothing, electrical machinery, furs and fur garments, glass and glassware, nonferrous metals and products, rayon yarn, and rubber;

[1] *Directory of Labor Unions in the United States*, Bulletin No. 937, U.S. Department of Labor, June 1948.

[2] Ibid.

in leather tanning, meat packing, newspaper printing, shipbuilding, basic steel and sugar refining, longshoring, shipping, metal mining, motion-picture production, and local and intercity trucking; and as actors and musicians, airline pilots and mechanics, brewery, local bus and street car, railroad, and telegraph workers.

Clearly, the individual worker is being immersed in an expanding association, over which he can have only decreasing control. The relationship of the worker to his union, and of the union to the larger community, has precipitated many public and private issues undreamed of by the laborers who established their first small locals. The powerful national union is replacing the individual, and we are faced with the prospect that there will soon be little personal bargaining left, and, by implication, small freedom of occupational choice. From the union's point of view, control of the competitive job, whether locally, as in building, or nationally, as in steel or shipping, became an essential of survival. It had to protect its members against the competing lower wages of the unorganized workers or run the risk of disintegration. In many industries—men's clothing, women's garments, coal, textiles, printing, and so on—the management of the organized plants or mines insisted that unionization be extended to include the plants of as yet unorganized competitors.

The workers' organizations could not have survived, and the organized plants would have gone bankrupt if it had proved impossible to extend the union rules and their consequent costs to a whole industry. The women's garment industry, for instance, although scattered throughout the entire country, has a central marketing structure, chiefly in New York, which brings distant cities into competition with each other.[3] Between 1910 and 1929 collective bargaining spread to every important market in the men's clothing industry, and to ninety-five per cent of all clothing manufacturers.[4] Lower wages in any market attracted employers from other cities. If the union was to preserve its gains in any one city, it had to extend itself to all of them.

Nation-wide organization has proved important for other reasons. The Amalgamated Clothing Workers Union has five or six social-security funds, of concern to half a million employees in six thousand plants. These contracts with organized associations or employers are on a national or area basis. Otherwise welfare plans would have to be negotiated separately six thousand times, and the welfare program would break down. Welfare plans, like wages and working conditions, could only be stabilized upon an industry-wide basis.[5]

A very similar experience is revealed by the Interna-

[3] *Hearings, I*, pp. 1334–5, "Statement of David Dubinsky, President of the International Ladies Garment Workers Union, A. F. of L., New York, N.Y.": "In addition to the New York manufacturers, most of the manufacturers who are located in other markets have show rooms in the city of New York where they display and sell their garments. Thus, manufacturers in New York, in Kansas City and in Los Angeles, in Boston and in Dallas, in Chicago and in Cleveland, are all in competition with each other. Economic reality forces the union to adopt a national wage policy to protect the workers throughout the country."

[4] *Hearings, II*, p. 404, "Statement of Hyman Blumberg, Executive Vice President of the Amalgamated Clothing Workers of America."

[5] Ibid., p. 412.

tional Ladies Garment Workers Union, which has a membership of over 380,000. It operates in 20 separate branches of the industry, has 452 locals in 265 cities scattered over 36 states. Its members are employed by more than 8,500 manufacturers, and its contractual relations embrace 90 employers' associations, as well as some 900 individual firms.[6] The relative stability enjoyed by this industry in recent years is due to the national union, to which employers have frequently appealed to police the contracts.[7]

The unions in the printing industry have for years written a pattern of nation-wide standards into their local contracts because "Neither industry nor we can afford competition to union working conditions, desirable as competition on other factors may be." [8] Individual haggling with each of the thousands of small printing shops proved impracticable and induced the desire for basic rules, nationally applicable. The Typographical Union has been working toward these ends since 1852.[9]

If conditions in the shipping industry are different from those already described, demands by workers for nationally uniform standards have proved no less insistent. The men working the ships on the seas have striven for equal wages and working conditions, and have discovered in the union hiring hall the essential instru-

[6] *Hearings, I*, p. 1331, "Statement of David Dubinsky, President of the International Ladies Garment Workers Union, A. F. of L., New York, N.Y."

[7] Ibid., p. 1338.

[8] *Hearings, II*, p. 384, "Statement of President Woodruff Randolph, of the International Typographical Union."

[9] Ibid., pp. 385–6.

ment for the fulfillment of their plans. When a ship captain wants a crew, he goes to the union hiring hall. "There is no other place to go." An attempt to upset the present arrangement "would see the greatest disruption in shipping we have ever seen in this country." [10] The reason is obvious enough:

> If each employer had to bargain with a union which represented only his employees, you would have the greatest multiplicity and variation of working terms. You would have men leaving one ship and going to another ship with different rates and conditions. You would have ships tied up alongside of each other in the same dock with different terms of employment for the same job. That sort of thing would create chaos.[11]

Competition in wages and working conditions is not acceptable to the union because varying standards would make it difficult to maintain an organization, and in some industries competition is not acceptable to the owners of individual plants because wage differentials would give their competitors undue advantage in the market. In industries composed of many small competitive units the pressure for wage uniformity seems irresistible, but wage uniformities hasten the movement toward a monopoly

[10] *Hearings before the Committee on Labor and Public Welfare,* U.S. Senate, 80th Congress, 1st Session, on S. 55 and S.J. Res. 22, and all other bills and resolutions referred to the Committee having the object of reducing industrial strife in the United States. Part 2, February 1947 (hereafter referred to as *Hearings, III*), p. 623, "Statement of Almon E. Roth, President, National Federation of American Shipping."

[11] Ibid., p. 624.

of labor. This trend is equally evident in industries dominated by powerful corporations.

In the telephone industry, for instance, the influence of the Bell system overrides the local telephone companies, and the union found that no local division of the telephone system could make changes in wages, hours, and labor conditions. The local company could not even have a distinctive classification of its employees. The organizational structure of each of the separate divisions was found to be like the others, and the separate plans for employees' pensions and disability and death benefits were alike and could not be changed without the consent of the unifying American Telephone and Telegraph Company. Under the circumstances, local bargaining proved self-defeating. Centralized control over management in the telephone industry made for industry-wide bargaining.[12]

The evidence, in fact, points toward a similar policy in General Motors:

> Our experience in General Motors demonstrates that the drive to establish more complete centralization of control on a corporation-wide basis, as opposed to control on the plant level, comes from the corporation rather than from the union. Efforts on the part of the union to obtain disposition of grievances and policy matters on the plant level have been and are rebuffed with the response that these matters must be dealt with by corporation officials in Detroit.[13]

[12] *Hearings*, *II*, p. 172, "Statement of Joseph A. Beirne, President, Communications Workers of America."

[13] *Hearings*, *I*, "Progress Report of the Chairmen to the Members

There is, therefore, ground for the statement that "It is the nature of the corporate structure which has determined the nature of the union structure." [14]

Similar trends toward uniformity are evidenced in textiles, where certain manufacturing units, because of their size, dominate labor relations for entire sections of the industry.

> Employer units in the textile industry are national in scope and their control is highly concentrated. American Thread Co. operates 10 plants located in 7 States; American Woolen Co. operates 25 plants located in 8 States; American Viscose Corp. operates 9 plants located in 4 States; Celanese Corp. operates 11 plants in 8 States; J. P. Stevens & Co. operates 35 plants in 8 States; United Merchants & Manufacturers operates 10 plants in 5 States; Textron Corp. operates 32 plants in 7 States; Burlington Mills operates 55 plants in 7 States. . . . These are but a few of the employers in the textile industry with whom TWUA deals. In some cases a single corporation owns and operates the entire chain. In others each plant is a separate corporation. In all cases labor-relations policies are directed by the centralized executive office.[15]

These examples suggest the union's problem. No local union in any one plant is competent to protect the interests of the workers, because an agreement with a major

---

of the Special Committee to Study Problems of American Small Business," p. 1315.

[14] Ibid., p. 1314.

[15] Ibid., p. 1522, "Statement of George Baldanzi, Executive Vice President, Textile Workers' Union of America, C.I.O."

operator influences the policies of other units in the industry. Effective implementation of union demands in these industries has waited upon regional or industry-wide unionization. In part, this has been made necessary by interlocking financial control. Single financial institutions have membership on the board of many competing units in the same industry.

"Rhode Island Hospital National Bank of Providence, R.I.; Old Colony Trust of Boston; National City Bank of New York; First National Bank of Greenville, N.C.; American Trust Co. of Charlotte, N.C., have representatives on literally over 100 different textile directorates." [16]

The national trade-union, however, is not merely a response to monopoly. It hastens the growth of larger industrial units. By its insistence upon similar or uniform standards, it increases the relative costs for the smaller plants and adds to their difficulties of survival in the face of competition from the larger corporations.

An almost classic example of these tendencies is offered by the behavior of the American Federation of Musicians in the motion-picture industry. The small producers in Los Angeles were compelled to accept the contract signed by the large ones. The union insisted that each producer engage a twenty-piece orchestra on a permanent two-year basis. If the producer did not need a permanent orchestra, he was required to hire a fifty-piece orchestra at a minimum of $25 an hour for each musician for no less than three hours any time he used a band. A

[16] Ibid., p. 1522.

company that had previously been able to meet its need for music for $240 now had a minimum expenditure of $3,750. The small companies, under duress, acquiesced in hiring a twenty-man orchestra for 52 weeks, at an annual cost of $16,900 per man. The band was under contract to play 520 hours during the year. The small companies, however, did not require a twenty-piece band, nor could they use 520 hours of music a year, but they were forced to pay for both, and for two weeks' vacation at full pay, in addition to the 52 weeks contracted for.[17]

In other words, small companies, which used to get along with eight men, now had twelve additional musicians forced upon them. "Every contract in the industry compels the employer to hire the number of 20 [musicians] for the number of hours determined, not by the employer, but by the representative of the union." [18] As the studios put it, "We are employing men . . . we don't want." [19] The contract of the major studios is forced upon the smaller ones because "they won't work for us" otherwise.

A similar story can be told for the radio industry. A broadcasting station in Los Angeles was compelled to pay $12,000 extra for using a national program already

[17] *Hearings before the Special Subcommittee of the Committee on Education and Labor*, House of Representatives, 80th Congress, 1st Session Pursuant to H. Res. 111. Hearings held June, July, and August 1947 (hereafter referred to as *Hearings, VI*), p. 76, "Testimony of Isaac E. Chadwick, President, Independent Motion Picture Producers Association, Los Angeles, Calif."

[18] Ibid., p. 76.

[19] Ibid., p. 77.

paid for because time differences between New York and California forced it to delay the program and play it from a recording.[20]

The American Federation of Musicians required the "Metropolitan stations where orchestras were available to expend 5½ per cent of their net income for staff orchestras," in spite of the fact that one of the local broadcasting companies using orchestras was losing money.[21] It required broadcasting companies to hire musicians even if they did not need them, and there are reports that some stations paid a stand-by orchestra for two years without their playing a single note. The Chicago musicians' local forced a minimum of eight stand-by musicians on radio stations, and mechanical devices had to be handled by members of the union. Similar practices were developed in other fields requiring musicians. The Shubert Lafayette Theatre was forced to hire six musicians, whom it did not want or need, at $525 a week, and upon refusal found that the stage hands would not work, and later that it could get no bookings unless it complied.

The Chicago local of the American Federation of Musicians tried to force the Chicago Opera House to take 29 musicians for an ice show when the regular orchestra of the house consisted of 8, and to pay for 10 performances for 9 shows at $25 a musician for each performance. The show was canceled.

When the Metropolitan Opera played in Chicago, a

[20] Ibid., p. 538, "Testimony of Lewis Allen Weiss, Executive, Mutual Broadcasting System and Don Lee Broadcasting System, Los Angeles, California."

[21] Ibid., p. 540.

stand-by conductor at $370 and 7 men at $189 a week were forced upon the theater. This same opera house had to hire a stand-by orchestra of as many musicians as a touring ballet company carried, 18 in number.[22]

The Los Angeles local of the American Federation of Musicians estimated the income and business of a theater, restaurant, or other house of entertainment, then decided how many musicians that enterprise had to take, and what wages it would have to pay, without previous consultation or agreement.

Such practices by a trade-union require complete authority over the labor in the industry. That power the American Federation of Musicians claims for itself. James C. Petrillo, the president of the union, believes that "Monopoly, so far as labor is concerned, is justifiable, because only in that way can the union become strong and increase wages of the workman and better his condition."[23] This monopoly rests on the following basis: Of the 216,000 members, approximately 32,000 earn their living exclusively as musicians. "About 86,400 have dropped their instruments," but have kept their cards for "sentimental reasons." Membership requirements are broadly elastic.[24] "Performers on musical instruments of any kind who render musical services for pay are classed as professional musicians" and are eligible for

[22] Ibid., p. 288, "Testimony of James C. Thompson, Operator of Chicago Opera House and Civic Theater, Chicago, Ill."

[23] *Hearings, IV*, p. 349, "Statement of James C. Petrillo, President, American Federation of Musicians."

[24] *Hearings, VI*, p. 568, "Interim Report (Pursuant to H. Res. 111). Report of Special Committee to Investigate James C. Petrillo. The American Federation of Musicians, et al."

membership. "Anyone over sixteen years [1946 Constitution, Article IX, Sec. 15, p. 57] who can play any instrument by ear or notes is eligible for membership."

These 32,000 regularly employed musicians have managed, through their organization, to acquire a degree of influence and dominion over the theater, orchestras, radio, moving pictures, and television that has in many ways limited the freedom of these groups.

On cross-examination on July 7, 1947, before the special Subcommittee on Education and Labor of the House of Representatives, Mr. Petrillo testified as follows: [25]

MR. PETRILLO: "Well, if our plans come out all right, you would not listen on the radio."

CONGRESSMAN FISCHER: "And you wouldn't listen on juke boxes."

MR. PETRILLO: "You wouldn't listen on the juke boxes."

CONGRESSMAN FISCHER: "You have a virtual monopoly over the making of music . . . in this country. . . ."

MR. PETRILLO: "I cannot deny it. . . ."

MR. MCCANN: "You have a contract with the major movies of the country depriving them of the right to use any sound track showing musicians or recording a musical performance." [26]

MR. PETRILLO: "And television."

MR. MCCANN: "And television?"

MR. PETRILLO: "Yes."

[25] *Hearings, VI*, p. 196.
[26] Ibid., p. 199.

MR. MCCANN: "And that contract exists for all of the movies of this country?"

MR. PETRILLO: "Yes."

The union can exercise these controls because all musicians working for a living with their instruments are members of the organization. And all musicians are members of the union because no one could earn a living by playing unless he was a member. This means, in effect, that a contract with the union is a license to operate.

The union had a closed-shop arrangement with all recording companies (somewhere between 550 and 600) so that it was impossible for anyone to make a single recording of his own.[27] Not a school, church, or choir could make a recording without permission. All of these recording contracts expired at the same time, and in 1942 the union decided to make no recordings or transcriptions. In 1944, recording companies were required to pay a ¼ cent royalty on a record selling for 35 cents, ½ cent for one selling for 50 cents, and ¾ for one selling at 75 cents. By the end of 1946 this royalty amounted to $2,600,000, and was estimated to have reached $3,000,000 in 1947. When the Taft-Hartley bill outlawed these payments, the union announced that there would be no more recordings.

The Chicago Sunday Evening Club, a voluntary religious organization of long standing, had to pay a stand-by musician because music was rendered by two volunteers who were not members of the union. Stand-by

[27] Ibid., p. 252, "Testimony of Rex Riccardi, Assistant to the President, American Federation of Musicians."

musicians had to be engaged in San Francisco for children playing on the radio.[28] In February 1945 the members of the American Federation of Musicians were prohibited from playing for television in any form until further notice. The Chicago elementary-school band was stopped from broadcasting over the city-owned station because it had no money for a stand-by orchestra. This also included school choirs.[29] In 1944 the national president of the union reported that in 1943 there was no school band or orchestra on the networks, "and there never will be without the permission of the American Federation of Musicians." [30] Special permission had to be secured from Mr. Petrillo to broadcast Mass from St. Patrick's Cathedral in New York on Christmas 1945,[31] to carry President Truman's Army Day speech in 1946 because it included incidental music,[32] and to send over FM and AM radio an Army recruiting program from Schenectady in July 1946.[33]

The 32,000 musicians making their living by playing an instrument, in their attempt to achieve economic security and a high wage for themselves, have brought the American Federation of Musicians into being. And this union, because it is a monopoly, has been able to

[28] Ibid.

[29] Ibid., p. 264, "Testimony of George Jennings, Director of Radio for the Chicago Public Schools, Chicago, Ill."

[30] Ibid., p. 273 (quoted from a statement of James C. Petrillo, January 1944).

[31] *Hearings, IV*, p. 95, "Statement of Leonard L. Asch, President and General Manager, Capitol Broadcasting System, Schenectady, N.Y."

[32] Ibid., p. 96.

[33] Ibid., p. 96.

restrict the development of the moving picture, radio, FM, television, and record-making. It has interfered with the broadcasting of private religious services, Army bands, school concerts over publicly owned broadcasting stations, the programing of music, whether popular or classical, and the ability to bring opera to distant cities, and has limited the musical education of the American people. It has influenced the flow of investment and enjoyment in a whole series of activities from restaurants to recording and juke boxes. All of this is a by-product of an attempt to protect a small number of musicians—"anyone who plays any instrument by ear or from notes" for a wage. And there are only 32,000 of them in the United States. The broadest type of national public policy has been decided by this union in response to the requirements of its own members without any apparent regard for the needs of the American people.

In its attempt to secure high wages and economic security, a union seeks to achieve monopoly, and then to use the monopoly for its own ends. The ends aimed at are not revolutionary in intent, but they are revolutionary in effect. The nature of the wage-and-price bargain has been completely changed. So, too, has the relationship of the individual worker to his fellows and to his employer. A third party, the union, has appeared upon the scene, and this third party, originally created by the workers to make their bargaining more effective, has now become so powerful that it has reduced both the worker (member) and the employer to a subordinate position. This is a logical and inevitable by-product of a series of simple objectives and honest endeavors. It is not a result of conspiracy or evil intent. To survive at all the union must achieve a monopoly over its resources (labor), and the monopoly, once achieved, takes the form of imposing upon the employer a wage bargain, "a price for labor," which in increasing instances he has to accept or go out of business. And if the shop or industry is small he goes out of business whether he accepts or not. In one instance the costs are too high; in the other he can get no labor.

The ability of either the worker or the employer to make a living has, in many instances, become permissive.[34] It depends upon the consent of the union. The employer and the individual worker are forced to accept the rules laid down by this third party. These rules are neither arbitrary nor capricious. They are devised with the best intent in the world, they are a response to an immediate

[34] *New York Times*, October 12, 1948: "LINEN SUPPLIER SAYS UNION BARS LAUNDRY. The Arrow Linen Supply Company of 1831 Second Avenue, charging that it faced financial ruin, brought an action in Supreme Court yesterday to lift an alleged laundry ban by a labor union. Named as defendants were the Amalgamated Clothing Workers of America, C.I.O., the Laundry Workers Joint Board of Greater New York and Local 331 of the union.

"Benjamin Jacobs, president of the company, said it started last May to supply linens to restaurants and clubs. He reported that Annapolis Laundry, Ltd., declared he would have to 'secure clearance' from the union.

"Mr. Jacobs related that at the joint board, he signed agreements and was told that 'everything was all set.' He was informed later by Annapolis that it no longer could do his work 'because the union had ordered them to stop work on our linens.'

"The plaintiff's head said there was no labor dispute and that he had conformed with all union regulations. He asserted that Annapolis was willing to handle his work if the union would lift the ban and that no other laundry would take the job because all had union contracts."

need, and they aim at giving to the individual economic security and a higher wage. The aim is laudable and morally right. The method is innocent: a refusal to work when it is against the worker's interest to do so. But the result is a monopoly, exercised by a third party, which modifies the older wage bargain. Moreover, this third party, a new institution called a union, develops interests and a logic of its own. The logic of the union is inconsistent with the previous institutional design, for, without malice aforethought, it destroys the basis upon which the older institutions rested. All unions are bent in the same direction.

In New York City, Local No. 3 of the International Brotherhood of Electrical Workers has complete dominion over the manufacture, wholesale distribution, sale, installation, and maintenance of all electrical equipment in construction work. The local has in the past used this grip to keep out of the New York City market electrical equipment made in other parts of the country, even if made by members of the same national organization. Local No. 3 of the I.B.E.W. has refused to handle the product of electricians belonging to the same union. It wished to operate in a closed market. The only condition under which the New York local would permit its members to work on material manufactured outside the city was first to dismantle and then rewire the equipment.[35]

[35] *Hearings before the Committee on Labor and Public Welfare*, U.S. Senate, 80th Congress, 1st Session, on S. 55 and S.J. Res. 22 and all other Bills and Resolutions Referred to the Committee Having the Object of Reducing Industrial Strife in the United States, Part I, January and February 1947, p. 178, "Statement of Robert Stafford Ed-

This is one instance of a local monopoly affecting manufactures beyond its own city. In the case of the steel workers' union we have an instance where an industry-wide wage policy weakens the economic position of the small plants. The small companies were forced to accept the wage settlement of the large companies. They found that in following the contract of the larger companies they were damaging their competitive position. But when they tried to argue their case, the local union committee informed them "that it had no authority to deviate in the least from the demands promulgated by the national headquarters." [36]

It is clear that the standard wage is deemed a prerequisite for achieving and maintaining a labor monopoly. To maintain it, trade-unions have employed many devices, among them the strike and the boycott. These same methods have been used by one union against another in efforts to secure exclusive dominion over the work force in shops, plants, or industries. Jurisdictional battles between unions are by no means infrequent, and this intramural strife has had a bearing upon increasing costs.

In mass-production industries, where tasks can be clearly defined, jurisdictional quarrels can be contained and work can go on. But in industries where every product requires a different alignment of tasks, and even the creation of new devices, the jurisdictional squabble can be-

---

wards, President, National Electrical Manufacturers Association, New York, N.Y."

[36] *Hearings, III*, p. 649, "Statement of A. V. Murray, President, Scaife Co., Oakmont, Pennsylvania."

come difficult and exasperating. In the moving-picture industry there are forty unions competing for the available jobs, and to whom the job belongs is a question that sometimes no one can decide, because no definition of the task is acceptable to all parties. A dispute, therefore, can arise any time of the day and over any activity: who should nail up a board; who should have the right to pull out the nails when the board has to come down; or who should fill a water bottle. These differences, petty in themselves, would be less aggravating if the men involved directly were the only ones who went out on strike. But the rule that union men must not cross a picket line generalizes every petty dispute into a major threat to tie up the plant, the studio, or the entire industry with its 30,000 workers.

The constant bickering, the seemingly endless quarrels between the different crafts, the lack of power on the part of the local unions to settle the issue of jurisdiction, and the special pride and privilege that each craft claims for itself have in the past made continuous operation difficult or impossible, while management is so harassed by the unforeseen but interminable squabbles that its morale is undermined. The unpredictable and seemingly irrational outbursts gravely affect the ability of management to carry on. The employer is an innocent bystander and has no available remedy.

An example of how jurisdictional disputes may affect a business enterprise is the testimony of a Hollywood motion-picture producer before a Congressional committee:

MR. FREEMAN: ". . . I think the producers in Hollywood had become threadbare by all of the problems that existed—by all of the conflict that was going on between the unions. . . . Go ahead. We are tired. We are worn out. There is no way ever to settle all of these conflicts that are existing.

"It made no difference what you did. You went home and the next morning you had another threat. If you went out to try to play a game of golf, you can rest assured there would be work stoppage in the studios, because—in one instance with us it was a water bottle."

MR. MCCANN: "Tell us about the water bottle. I would like to hear about it."

MR. FREEMAN: "The water bottle was empty on the set and one fellow started to put the filled water bottle back into the stand. They called a stoppage because he didn't have jurisdiction over the water bottle.

"They had to send out for a laborer somewhere way out on a back lot for the laborer to put in the water bottle. They were all thirsty and couldn't work until they got a drink, so the laborer had to put the water bottle in the empty stand." [37]

Another witness testified: "We had a work stoppage" over "one board . . . 3 feet long requiring four nails, so I said 'Well, go ahead, boys, you nail them down!' Laborers tore out those four nails and I said to the other

[37] *Hearings before a Special Subcommittee of the Committee on Education and Labor*, 80th Congress, House of Representatives, 1st Session, Pursuant to H. Res. 111, Volume 1, Hearings held at Los Angeles, California, August and September 1947, pp. 107–8, "Testimony of Young Frank Freeman, Vice President, Paramount Pictures, Inc., Hollywood, Calif."

faction, 'Put those same four nails back in. . . .' We have those things, too numerous to mention." The increased cost has been placed by one studio at 180 per cent, and another says: "We run 1,200 and 1,300 per cent" over the previously budgeted costs."[38]

Thus, in its attempt to protect the job security of its members, the union, by increasing the costs of the small producer and the small businessman in general, has tended to strengthen the very power of monopoly to which it presumably is opposed. In his efforts to regain security and "social identity" in an unstable economy and an atomized society, the worker has raised a powerful and growing institution that increasingly restricts the industry he works in, and circumscribes the life of the workers who earn their living at it.

The essence of the conflict is union power, because without it the union could not survive, and the necessary logic of the situation requires that it always increase it. This conflict over power within the economy has community-wide implications. The search is always for greater security, the method is always increased power for setting up standards of economic life that will stabilize the job and, by implication, the economy. The effects have always been increasing limitation of freedom of action, and an increasing trend toward equality of income. The trade-union and the older range of competitive freedoms are incompatibles.

The free market of the businessman, by constant pressure for lower costs or a secured price, tends toward

[38] Ibid., p. 111.

monopoly. The free market for labor, by a constant pressure for pecuniary security and higher wages, leads in the same direction. In fact, both industry and labor in a world of free competition lead toward monopoly. This monopoly may not soon become "perfect," but the tendency toward its perfection is always there. Historically, the ideal of a free competitive world, where each man by himself is a representative of the implicit harmony of the whole, has proved a snare and a delusion, and self-defeating. Both labor and capital, when given the choice, have "escaped from freedom" and bartered away their privileges for the hope of security.[39]

[39] The reader may gather some comfort from the following reflections of a famous historian: "Like the clergy and like the nobility, the middle class was itself a privileged order. It formed a distinct legal group and the special law it enjoyed isolated it from the mass of the rural inhabitants which continued to make up the immense majority of the population. Indeed, as has already been seen, it was obliged to preserve intact its exceptional status and to reserve to itself the benefits arising therefrom. Freedom, as the middle class conceived it, was a monopoly." Henri Pirenne: *Medieval Cities* (Princeton University Press, 1925), p. 221.

CHAPTER IX

Contract versus Status

TRADE-UNIONISM, as we have seen, has forced a structural change in our industrial society. This change is world-wide in character. While there are important variations in different areas, the similarities are everywhere apparent. A new pattern of industrial relations has come into being, recognizable for what it is all over the industrial world. It is just as recognizable as the corporation, the trust, or the cartel.

With this change, collective bargaining has become a means of adjusting the day-to-day issues between labor and management. The question raised over and over again is whether collective bargaining is compatible with the protection of the consumer, the maintenance of "full employment," the increase of production, the continuance of technological improvements, the narrowing of the swing between deflationary and inflationary tendencies, the defending of job security, and the protection of the individual against the loss of those freedoms so essential to a democratic way of life. All of these issues, basic to our times, have become involved in the attempt of the individual worker to achieve "economic security."

This is inevitably so because, as the Webbs pointed out, "Collective bargaining . . . implies in its fullest development compulsory Trade Unionism."[1] The vehicle for compulsory trade-unionism is union security, and in 1945 "approximately 77 per cent of all wage earners covered by collective agreements were covered by agreements containing union-security provisions."[2] Union security is insisted upon because without it "a union cannot exist and cannot maintain itself as an effective collective bargaining force on behalf of the workers."[3] When given the choice, the workers accept union security by an overwhelming majority. Out of ten thousand elections for the union shop, which is the original form of union security, "98 per cent . . . were won by the unions."[4] Effective collective bargaining implies that membership in a trade-union becomes a prerequisite to securing a job. The force of this statement is little changed by the various kinds of union security written into the agreement: the closed shop, maintenance of membership, or the union hiring hall. The fact is that "Job control is passing from the employer to the union."[5]

[1] Sidney and Beatrice Webb: *Industrial Democracy*, p. 533.

[2] *Hearings, II*, p. 51, "Statement of Paul M. Herzog, Chairman of the National Labor Relations Board."

[3] *Hearings, I*, p. 1224, "Statement Submitted by the International Longshoremen's and Warehousemen's Union before the Senate Committee on Labor and Public Welfare."

[4] *Hearings, II*, p. 7, "Statement of Hon. Gerald W. Landis, Representative in Congress from the State of Indiana."

[5] T. R. Witmer: "Civil Liberty and the Trade Union," *Yale Law Review*, Vol. L, p. 624.

As long as the union can limit the number of workers it will admit, and insist upon membership as a condition of receiving or keeping a job, it can control the workers within the industry. The courts, under the common law, have upheld the right of the unions to exclude new members on the grounds that they are voluntary associations.[6] But they are voluntary associations with compulsive powers over both the employer and the worker. They are, in fact, private lawmaking bodies whose rules affect the lives of millions of human beings and thousands of industrial plants. This is evidenced by the more than fifty thousand collective labor agreements existing in the country. The unions that sign these contracts acquire an influence over the activities of their members which in time circumscribe their daily lives and redefines the privileges of men who, under the law, are equal to each other. Without intent or plan, the trade-union movement is integrating the workers into what in effect amounts to a series of separate social orders. It is re-creating a society based upon status and destroying the one we have known in our time—a society based upon contract.[7]

[6] R. A. Newman: "The Closed Union and the Right to Work," *Columbia Law Review*, Vol. XLIII, p. 45.

[7] " 'Our forefathers,' said the Emperor Sigismund in 1434, 'have not been fools. The crafts have been devised for this purpose that everybody by them should earn his daily bread, and nobody shall interfere with the craft of another. By this the world gets rid of its misery, and everyone may find his livelihood.' 'The first rule of justice,' said the Parliament of Paris three hundred and fifty years later, 'is to preserve to every one what belongs to him: this rule consists not only in preserving the rights of property, but still more in preserving those belonging to the person which arise from the prerogative of birth and of position.' 'To give to all subjects indiscriminately,' argued on

If membership in a union is essential to an opportunity to work, and if every union has its own rules of admission, apprenticeship, dues, initiation fees, promotion, wages, retirement funds, and social benefits, then every union becomes in effect a differentiated order within the community, endowing its own members with rights and immunities shared only among themselves. Moreover, a member finds it increasingly difficult to leave his union, because the penalties for desertion are severe. These penalties include the loss of a job, the impossibility of securing other employment in the same industry, the loss of seniority and possible promotion, and the surrender of accumulated retirement, sickness, and old-age benefits. A new body of rights and disciplines, which greatly change the substance of a free society, has come into being. A single bargaining agency collects dues (its own form of taxation) from the worker, without his consent, through the check-off, and has enforceable union security provisions so that the worker must end by being a member of the union. In the spread of such industry-wide agreements we have the making of a new social design in which status rather than contract is the governing rule.

In theory, this status is voluntarily assumed. In fact, the penalties for not accepting the "voluntary" status become unavoidable. This compulsory membership is now to be found in a vast number of industries, occupations, and professions, from barbers to steelworkers, from

---

that occasion the eminent Advocate-General Séguier, 'the right to hold a store or to open a shop is to violate the property of those who form the incorporated crafts.' " Webb, op. cit., pp. 565–6.

musicians to airplane pilots, from chorus girls to sailors. Skilled and unskilled, professional and learned occupations, small and large plants, highly mechanized and semi-mechanized industries, are being incorporated into and made part of this pattern, and there is no prospect of an immediate end to the movement. If the history of trade-unionism demonstrates anything at all, it is that restrictive legislation, or other opposition, which proved ineffectual when the movement was new will not bring it to a halt now.

It is noteworthy that the growth of these stratifications has been justified and defended in the name of freedom, equality, and justice. The freedom, equality, and justice here spoken of have a functional rather than a political or civil context. One of the long-run and unforeseen byproducts of the individual worker's attempt to achieve "economic security" is the gradual remolding of industrial society on the older order of "estates." The Industrial Revolution destroyed a social system in which each man had a place in a "society" and in which he could fulfill his role as a human being. It gradually tore that "society" apart and robbed man of his traditional responsibilities and duties. But membership within a social group, so necessary to man, reappeared in a new form when the workers were congregated into industries. Here a common setting made the strangers of yesterday the companions of today. All that has followed in the structure and impact of the trade-union movement was a necessary sequence to the organic relationship the factory imposed. The industrialism that destroyed a society of status has now re-created it. The last one hundred and fifty years are a strange interlude in the history of man in the Western World, a period in which man was "freed" from one age-old association and, after a lapse, gradually reidentified with another one. If there is anything to this view of the matter, the system of "estates" now being developed is a necessary and logical outcome of the Industrial Revolution.

The process is obscured because, like every "society," the trade-union serves many ends. Its conscious purpose can be given formal embodiment in a constitution and rules, but there are also the unforeseeable by-products that arise out of associated activity. Like life itself, a trade-union is creative in character, and largely unpredictable in outcome. The rules a union makes for its own government are, like municipal law, equally applicable to all the associates, and are essential to the survival of the group as such. But the written rules are only the formal part of the governing law; there is also the unwritten law, the mores of the group, and the constitution becomes something to be applied within the special milieu created by common experience. This unwritten law is vaguely definable by the sense of what seems right and proper to the group as a whole. A body of loyalists, values, rights, duties, privileges and immunities, tolerances and expectancies, as between members and nonmembers, makes itself felt and conditions the enforcement of the written rules embodied in the constitution. Every union develops its slogans and symbols, its special sense of separateness and identity. It is this body of vague but affective tradition that defines the character of the union and assures its existence. If the union merely lived by its constitution and bylaws, it would have little vitality, and its life would be both troubled and short. It is the organic cohesiveness of the union that has given it its role in the modern world.

In addition to the union's own laws, written and unwritten, there are the rules that govern the relationships between union and industry. Whether there is a collective agreement or not, there is an undefined body of "law" that describes the relationship between workers and management. That is true even if there is no formal organization, for the group exists before the union is organized, and its mere existence implies a body of half-conscious, half-assumed rights and obligations. An unwritten law pervades the relationships between labor and management long before the union comes into being. The only alternative would be chaos and dissolution. The emergence of the union merely formalizes the existing group.

When the trade-union and the management sign a collective agreement, they set up a means for implementing and developing what has been called "industrial jurisprudence." But this "jurisprudence" was there from the time the workers first cohered into a group under the common discipline of the factory. The collective agreement, therefore, is the embodiment of the already existing rules and privileges.

The collective agreement is not primarily an instrument of industrial peace. It is rather a means for bringing under an accepted "common-law" procedure the issues over which friction arises. The end is not industrial quietude; that is not to be had. The end is an acceptable rule for dealing with the inevitable friction. The objective —the only possible objective—is a system of rules that make for the continuance of peaceful friction over the differences that arise a thousand times a day in any concern. The end is to make strikes unnecessary by confining the friction within a body of "common law" to which both sides subscribe.

The collective agreement, therefore, becomes the instrumentality for adapting the accepted rules to changing needs. But the sum of the expanding rules adds up to a reduction of the area governed by contract, and an expansion of the area in which men's lives are ruled by status. The innocent method of this great transformation is collective bargaining, and the growing "law" of this new society is the union-management agreement. By its mere existence the collective labor agreement is a denial of the older concept of free labor. The collective agreement is the substance out of which a society of status is being constructed brick by brick, stone by stone. The edifice, if not completed, is well advanced and visible in its broad outlines. The collective agreement records the rules of the game as it is developing between management and labor. The game remains the same, but the rules are always multiplying and becoming more inclusive because each collective agreement builds upon the last. What seemed new yesterday becomes a matter of course today, and the new rule merely advances the position that the trade-union occupied up to now. The "industrial jurisprudence" that has come to rule the relationship between the workers and their employers is expanding, and must expand, as more and more people are forced to depend upon a wage for all of their living and for all of their security.

Therein lies the root both of the society of status that the trade-union is forging and of the planned society that the welfare state would forge if the centrifugal forces embodied in trade-unionism do not make it both unnecessary and impossible. The growing dependence upon a money wage has made men increasingly dependent upon some outside agency in periods of helplessness and crisis. As long as men had the greater part of their living in real income produced by themselves, the uncertainties of the money wage could be tolerated. The minimum requirements of food, shelter, and care in times of sickness and old age, in infancy and childhood, in the emergency of death and misfortune, could be, and were, provided. The procurement of a real income was and had to be either a family or a community effort. Either the community or the family acted as the natural social-security agency for the fatherless, the aged, and the weak. The greater the dependence upon a real income, the larger was the role of the family and the community. The heavier the dependence on a money wage, the fuller became the individualization, equality, and isolation of each member of the family and each member of the group.

When the time arrived in our urbanized industrial society when a money wage came to represent the sole income for the mass of individuals, it carried with it not only complete independence and isolation, but also complete helplessness against the vicissitudes and needs that each individual faces at some time in his life. The freedom and individualism made possible by the full substitution of a money income for all other income inevitably destroyed the extended family as well as the parochial community. The free, but helpless, individual fell back upon either the trade-union or the state. The needs of childhood, widowhood, old age, and invalidism could not now be met by either the family or the parish. They had, in fact, both ceased to function as effective social-security institutions. Something else was required, and the only available means of satisfying the demands made by human helplessness fell by default to the union and to its chief competitor, the state. Public and private charity failed because they were the means for meeting the partial needs of a people largely cared for by an economy in which real income was the basis of the daily life of the people. Under those conditions "insecurity" was only partial, and mainly affected those who for some reason had lost the precious resource of membership in an extended family or in a parish. The mass of the people did not "fall" upon charity. The children and the aged were looked after at home or in the parish because there was a home and a parish. The money wage as the only source of life destroyed both the home and the parish. The insecurity suddenly became universalized because the money wage is precarious and unstable, and also because the children, the helpless widows, the sick, and the old, not to speak of the unemployed, cannot and do not earn a money wage. All men and women begin as infants, and an increasing proportion are now ending their lives aged and helpless, beyond the competence to earn a money wage.

The welfare state is the present response to this pressing situation. This new policy has come into focus because individual insecurity has been generalized in an ever expanding circle. The trades union became aware of this need long ago, before the state became conscious of the gravity of the situation, because it was concerned with people whose lives depended upon a money wage for all of their income.

The assumption of the economist that a competitive society, in which each person haggled his competencies in the market, is a good and wholesome thing tended, and still does tend, to obscure the difficulties of our modern society. A society in which all men have a money wage as their only resource is a society of very great complexity and full of hazards to the working of the economy itself. It is also a society in which all men become subject to the threat of insecurity, for which as individuals they have no remedy. The growing recognition of a universalized insecurity explains the proposal for a general one hundred dollars a month pension to the aged, proposed by Republican Senator Ives. It also explains President Truman's "Fair Deal," the socialism of the British Labour Party, and much of the increasing demands of the trade-unions.

The recent demands for old-age, sickness, and retirement pensions are the logical sequence to the disappearance of any source of real income for the mass of men in our urbanized industrial community. These demands were inevitable. The real question is not whether they will be met, but whether they will be met by trade-unions and industry or by the welfare state out of taxation.

The unions were both so weak and so slow that the larger need has caught up with them before the full tradition of security through industry and union could be universalized. Otherwise it might have been possible to protect society from the evil benefits of the welfare state. One thing is clear: a complete dependence upon a money-wage income for all, or even for the vast majority of men, can only end in tyranny by the state that provides the needed security, for to provide the security it will not only tax the substance of the community savings, but also interfere in the operation of our industrial society to lessen the unemployment and friction that complexity makes possible and perhaps inevitable. To save man from insecurity, the state will in time, as the increasing dependence of the individual forces it to, assume greater control over production, and over the members of the community itself, so as to regulate and make efficient the "welfare" that it will have to provide.

These unlooked-for consequences of complete dependence upon a money income may not explain the conscious justification of the protagonists of the welfare state. They, too, are blind and helpless victims of the efficiencies of a competitive society that has as its ideal an increasing income, expressed in money wages, for the mass of men. They, too, are caught in the consequent complexities of our society, over which they have no control and with which they meddle like blind mice gnawing at a rope that will spring the trap. They are not morally culpable, their intent is good, and their purposes of the highest. In fact, they cannot be blamed for the evil they would remedy, nor for the methods they would adopt.

Our milieu requires increased efficiency in production. Increased division of labor follows this demand, and increased dependence upon a roundabout way of gaining one's living is the inevitable result of the process. This indirect way—getting your food in a restaurant rather than at home, in buying bread rather than baking it, sending your shirts to the laundry rather than having the wash done in the home—is "efficient," but requires a larger income in money. It adds to the complexity of the society, to the helplessness of the individual, and makes for the inevitable insecurity. The personal insecurity this process produces fosters the growing demands of the trade-unions and explains the responsibilities of the welfare state. If the workers do not succeed in making the industry and the union the vehicle for the provision of essential security, then the state will perform the task. In the process it will destroy the liberties of our time and make man subservient to an all-absorbing Leviathan. If the trade-union succeeds in doing it, it will re-create a society of status, where the rule of the larger community law may survive as a means of protecting the individual against paying too heavy a price for the security he is given by the union. Under such conditions, a division of power will make possible the survival of the sense of independence, which the welfare state would ultimately destroy, with the best intent in the world and in the name of freedom.

What the trade-union is doing it has to do. It must add to its responsibilities for the individual, and place upon industry the responsibility for the welfare of its members. Only thus will it save both the union and the industry, even if that was not its conscious purpose. True enough, the older competitive structure is perhaps being undermined, but it is being undermined anyway, if not by the union, then by the corporation and by the state. The state must assume the responsibilities abandoned by the helpless family, the impoverished church, and the weakened parish if the industry and the union will not accept them.

In meeting the challenge of an all-consuming money economy the union has found in the collective agreement the essentially flexible instrument that it can use for the increasing security needs of its members. But two things should be noted: the growing demands reflect growing needs and expectancies; the collective agreement builds upon precedent rather than upon principle or doctrine. It does not attempt to write a theory into the law; it is creating a law out of innumerable precedents and judgments upon particulars. It would be a mistake to assume that each collective agreement rests upon some unique principle. The collective agreements vary in detail, and have greatly expanded the number of items of which they take cognizance, but they have changed little in basic commitment. These agreements began, and have remained, a collective rather than a personal effort to deal with the difficulties of our time as they impinge upon the laborer. This can be seen in what every collective labor agreement does and must attempt to do.

Previously the individual laborer could be discharged at will and without notice, but under collective bargaining:

1. The agreement has a time limit.
2. It has a previous body of minimum conditions, both legal and customary in "industrial jurisprudence" and precedent.
3. It is universalized so as to cover more than one person, more than any one group, shop, or factory.
4. It has objectives not immediately connected with the job, such as equalization of opportunities for union members.
5. It limits the rights and opportunities of others not embraced in the agreement.
6. It describes the expectancies for all members working in the shop and for all who will work in it.
7. It accepts the union as a going concern, and recognizes it as an agent of the workers, possessed of power to interfere in the industry.
8. It accepts the internal rules of the union as part of the contract; for instance, to discharge a man who loses his trade union membership.
9. It projects into the future the benefits of the im-

mediate agreement: unemployment, health, and old-age insurance.

10. It recognizes the "right" of the worker to his job.

11. It makes that right in some sense negotiable: displacement wage and retirement wage, depending upon the years employed.

12. It defines and universalizes privileges such as vacations with pay.

13. It regulates the future career of the individual within the industry by seniority.

14. It stratifies the relationships among individuals within the union as to pay, promotion, retirement.

15. It provides for "legal" redress through shop committees, arbitration, impartial chairmen.

16. It assumes a growing body of "industrial jurisprudence."

17. It ties the wage contract to some outside standard, such as price changes, productivity, profits, higher standard of living.

18. It sets rules for admission into the industry: age, apprenticeship, membership in the union.

19. It staggers work during slack periods, and increasingly imposes other such limitations upon management.

20. It contains provisions for penalizing employer, employee, and the union.

21. It provides for an internal judiciary system.

22. It establishes an increasing body of rights that go with the job, not with the worker.

23. It endows the union with powers of government, and an increasing responsibility to both the members and the industry.

These principles were implicit in the very first labor-management agreement. The specific items that creep into the agreements as they are renewed are a matter of precedent, convenience, and relative power. These rights and immunities are not interchangeable between one trade-union and another trade-union. Once a worker's lot is cast in one union and one industry, it becomes increasingly difficult for him either to alter his relative status in his own new "society," or to move from the union that has defined his role for him into another union where perchance he might discover a more congenial place for himself.

The worker, in fact, is caught up in a system that circumscribes both his mobility and his opportunities. Petrillo expressed the substance of the matter when he said: "I don't know where he [the expelled musician] would get a job today. An expulsion is a very serious matter for a man who is making his living with his instrument." [8] Expulsion is "a very serious matter" because it deprives the worker of the status that he had acquired, without restoring to him the opportunity for an individual contract. That opportunity no longer exists over broad areas of our society.

[8] *Hearings, IV, before the Committee on Education and Labor*, House of Representatives, 80th Congress, 2nd Session, on Restrictive Union Practices of the American Federation of Musicians, Vol. I, p. 343, hearings held at Washington, D.C., January 1948, "Statement of James C. Petrillo, President, American Federation of Musicians."

CHAPTER X

Power and Responsibility

THE EXPANDING power of labor unions makes possible, even probable, an integration on this new foundation of the greater part of the working and professional population. A new form of group identification and loyalty is being developed, a new kind of discipline is being accepted, and a special type of influence is making itself felt. These broad changes in law, loyalty, and discipline are peculiarly indifferent to ideological formulas and but little influenced by "radical" doctrines, the "reactionary" union being just as self-centered, dogmatic, exacting, and "revolutionary" as the "radical" one. The unions' historical significance lies in their impact upon social structure, not in their public utterances. Nor have these changes visibly affected the ordinary man's beliefs, ideas, and loyalties. The real meaning of the metamorphosis seems beyond the ken of either the members or the leaders of the trade-unions, who are the instruments of the transformation we are witnessing. As a matter of record, both the members and their leaders stand committed to all the beliefs and doctrines that the movement is making inoperative.

One consequence of this drift, long in the making, has recently begun to cause public concern. That is the power of a single strategically placed trade-union to disrupt the workings of our complex economy and to cast a shadow over society as a whole. A national strike by the railroad workers, if it were to last long enough, would prove disastrous to the whole economy, throw millions of workers out of their jobs, bring transportation to a halt, cast cities into darkness, stop ships from sailing the seas, and condemn the residents of thousands of small and large cities to starvation. In fact, our society, at least theoretically, could be strangled by any one powerful union. This great power held by one man or a few is greater than that previously exercised by any other person or group. It is greater than was claimed by the head of any state, and was seen only in special areas as a result of total war. This implied threat over a total society, which would, in addition, affect our military defense as well as our ability to carry on peaceful international relations, is in its nature absolute power. Even the union leaders seem but dimly aware of the threat to the nation as a whole contained in their ability to call a national strike.

It is in the nature of the trade-union movement to concentrate such powers in numerous vulnerable spots in our economy. A national coal strike would be of the same order as a railroad strike.[1] An electrical strike that

[1] It is interesting to note that John L. Lewis doubts that this power could be so used:

would still the powerhouses of the nation, or even the strike of only a small fraction of the working force of a great industry, such as the switchmen on the railroads, would have the same effect for the nation as a whole. Similar powers are concentrated locally. The few tugboat men in the harbor of New York City could deprive it of food and coal; the one thousand lathers could bring all building to a halt in that city and throw thousands of other workers out of their jobs. The milk-wagon drivers can endanger the sick in the hospitals, and elevator operators in the large public office buildings can disrupt vast national and international operations. The exercise of power under these conditions becomes irresponsible and, in practice, intolerable. It is irresponsible because the damage it does to the innocent victim, the community, is out of proportion to the gains achievable by the parties to the dispute. The fact that in a given instance the threat may mean the disruption of the community makes the exercise of such power intolerable. What needs to be repeated is that the impact of these new powers is a *con-*

"I want to point out that the Nation has never yet starved, frozen, or died from want of water. The restraints as affecting labor are the inherent restraints that affect all America. We have no guaranties in our country what a school board will do or a city council or a State legislature, or the Federal Congress, or a labor union, or the Baptist Church, or some other church, or the Kiwanis Club, or the Farm Federation. We have no guaranties that those organizations will not act wrongfully." *Hearings before the Committee on Labor and Public Welfare.* U.S. Senate, 80th Congress, 1st Session, on S. 55 and S.J. Res. 22, and all other bills and resolutions referred to the Committee having the object of reducing industrial strife in the United States, Part 4, March 1947 (hereafter referred to as *Hearings, V*), p. 1993, "Statement of John L. Lewis, President, United Mine Workers of America."

sequence of labor organization and not the original purpose.

We have here a curious outcome of the free market that began by describing labor as an impersonal, fluid, pecuniary, unmoral commodity. The theory neglected the fact that the laborer went with the labor that was hired. It failed to foresee that the morally associative relationship man needed would force him to contrive a union in self-defense, the long-run consequence of which, among many others, is the accumulation of power to disrupt the society itself. The willingness of union leaders to use their authority to call a national strike lies partly in the fact that the significance of the power they hold has not fully dawned upon them, and partly in the present-day situation, which balances a national union against a national industry.

Even more important is the casting of the conflict between management and labor in pecuniary terms. The definition of the issues at stake as the prospects of profits on one side and wages on the other makes possible the disruptive pattern of behavior when no agreement can be reached. That the argument should take this pecuniary form is a hangover from the day of a presumptively free, impersonal, and fluid market for both labor and ownership. The very existence of the corporation, the trust, the cartel, and the national or international union is evidence that the free market has been greatly circumscribed. The ideas that the free-market theory generated, and the motives it sanctioned, are still operative on both sides. This is evidenced by the requirement of such a dramatic threat as a national coal strike to call to mind that the structure has now so changed that even the language of an older day no longer applies.

That language and the ends it sanctioned ruled the scene for over a hundred years, and led the worker to take over the "business mores" of the competitive market. The description of trade-unionism as "business unionism" merely indicates that the workers adhered to the philosophy of the free market seriously enough to act upon it, and to try to get out of the situation every bit of pecuniary advantage that the traffic would bear. They wanted more wages, more benefits, shorter hours of labor, less responsibility, less work, more security. They wanted an increasing share of the total product of industry without committing themselves to a greater responsibility for providing the product. As they understood it, that was the economic ethics of the time. Get as much as you can; give as little for it as possible. They attempted to operate in a "sellers' market" and to enjoy the extra pecuniary advantages of a monopoly. Having lost a personal concern in the industry, having no proprietary interest, being subject to call and hire, and living in a world where larger pecuniary income was represented as the proper end of economic behavior, they behaved accordingly. The important point, however, is not their emphasis upon increased pecuniary reward for their labor. The real point is the insistence that this increase should go hand in hand with a lesser concern for the sources of production that made the increasing return possible.

One need not impugn the motives of the workers or

their leaders. The issues at stake were originally defined by the business ethics of the age. The "morals" of competitive business have lent themselves to the perversions of getting rich quick, to the notion of making money, of having a good job, meaning easy and highly remunerative. The trade-unions may not have taken over all of the implicit value judgments of the free market economy or have been aware of all its sanctions, but they took over those that they understood and that they could use. The real danger in this situation lies not in wanting an increasing share of the product, but in refusing to be responsible for producing the increased share. It lies in demanding an income from an industry without assuming a responsible relation to the industry. It lies in behaving as fluid, impersonal ownership behaves, which flows from industry to industry as the market dictates, from hour to hour, from day to day. A system in which neither the worker nor the owner has any effective moral concern for the industry that is the source of their living lacks the principle of survival.

The prospect of an escape from the evils of irresponsibility is to be found in the trade-union's challenge to managerial prerogatives. The claim to a participation in management is not expressed in these terms, but it has these effects and is an unconscious surrender of an irresponsible attitude by the unions. Management is a responsible function. It is, under present conditions, more responsible than ownership. When the unions press to share the managerial function, they are asking to be allowed to assume the responsibility that goes with management. They are doing that even if they are not aware of the commitment they are making, and even if they deny they are making it. That is why the argument over the separate prerogatives of management and trade-unions is largely beside the point. There is no line that can be drawn between the two spheres of interest, except at a single moment in a given industry. The situation is fluid, and will remain so. Neither the workers nor the management can define their relative positions in final terms. In fact, the very appearance of a trade-union is a denial of the unchallenged authority of the management. A union, by assuming responsibility for the welfare of its members and acting as their agent, must of necessity be concerned over every item that affects their fortunes. Every activity of management bears upon the well-being of the workers. The disputes at any moment are over a temporary delineation of a moving line. The end is participation by the trade-union in all of the affairs of management. Otherwise the trade-union would resign its responsibility for the governance of its members. That it cannot do without signing its death warrant. It must either push for increasing power and influence or begin to disintegrate.

This seems to emphasize conscious motivation, which is not the real drive behind the expanding concern over the issues of management. Actually, the union is being pushed toward more participation in an increasing range of managerial activities by its original commitment to stabilize the security of its members. Its responsibilities increase with its growing powers. If the union agreed to a permanent limitation of its field of activities, it would admit that it was an intruder and an outsider in the industry. But it is neither an outsider nor an intruder; it is part of the industry. It is the other side of management. The issue is not the degree to which it will participate in or substitute for management, but rather how constructive and fruitful its participation will prove. The real question is the feasibility of labor-union participation in management without destroying the efficiency and the productivity of industry. That is a very different matter from the artificially described body of rights that presumably "belong" only to one side of the productive organization. The trade-union movement cannot be understood unless it is accepted as a matter of course that the welfare of the industry is as much the concern of the organized workers as it is of management or of ownership.

The worker, once organized and integrated into the industrial structure, tends to surrender his freedom to separate himself from the industry. The union increasingly ties the worker to the industry and tends to convert a contract terminable at will into one terminable only at death. His union gives him his freedoms within the industry, but it hedges his "freedom" to abandon the industry within which he makes his living.

The developing situation is lost sight of in the persistent argument over wages, as if the union were chiefly occupied with pecuniary income. That is not the case. The overemphasis of economic ends has obscured the real issues. The economic ends are there, but there are also the purposes embraced by membership in a "society," and these include the broad ethical objectives that define the good life. The form the argument between management and labor takes is in some ways irrelevant to the inner bent of the union. Each dispute is over a specific issue. The underlying drive is increased participation in management, because whatever management does has its bearing not merely upon the future economic security of the members and the future role of the union, but also upon the undefinable but very real sense of membership in a going concern. The union may talk the language of the market and be obsessed by economic objectives. That is part of the milieu as given, and it is a language that both labor and management understand. But the underlying theme is the drive for moral status within the industry. A commitment to spend one's life in a job where no moral status was achievable would not be tolerable; it would be equivalent to slavery.

The union, if it is to survive, must maintain the fealty of its members, and it can do that only by giving them a sense of dignity and standing, not only within the union, but also within the industry. Such a sense of dignity can only be had if the workers have a concern for all the issues and difficulties of the enterprise. Identity on both a moral and a psychological basis is a condition of peaceful friction within the industrial system, and cannot be had as long as the workers and their unions are treated as outsiders. It is this underlying necessity that shapes the continuing pressure for increased participation in management. In gradually expanding the range of its responsibilities, the union satisfies the only irreducible expectancy of the worker: a growing moral status within the industry. The union thus gives the worker something he must have, a place in which he can feel at home; and only by doing this can the union be sure of that loyalty of its members which it must have to survive.

It is this moral adhesion of its members that has made it possible for the trade-union to challenge and defeat the corporation. The corporation never achieved the moral adhesion of those whose lives it ruled, and it failed to secure that devotion because it did not represent a moral purpose to which men could be loyal. It was a great power, resting upon the overstressing of economic ends, but subsisting within a moral vacuum. It gave men no faith to live by and no credo they would die for, and therefore nothing that they would in the long run accept. The corporation was not a family, a society, a church. Profit, the end of the corporation, is insufficient to stabilize the lives and satisfy the needs of men, and it evokes no absolute loyalty. The corporation rested upon economic power and brought its servants' attachment for cash, and that was insufficient.

It is no accident that the trade-union has a greater claim for approbation in our time, for, in spite of its shortcomings, it has a moral purpose and has given its members dignity and self-respect. It has attached to itself the blind loyalty of men for more than a hundred years, a loyalty that has survived persecution and poverty. The union has called into being a loyalty among its adherents that on more than one occasion accepted the challenge to battle in which men gladly risked their lives so that the union might survive. Workers, many of them, in the last hundred and fifty years, gave their lives so that their claim to self-respect and dignity, which they discovered in the union, should not be denied to them.

The specific matters in dispute between labor and management are incidents in a process. Agreement on one contentious issue merely raises another. The unions began intruding upon the prerogatives of management as soon as they were organized, organization itself being an intrusion, perhaps the most important single challenge in the history of industrial relations. All of the other issues that have come to the surface have rested upon the previous existence of the union. In the century-old conflict the workers' organizations have multiplied the items over which they have sought to establish a union rule.

This is illustrated in the case of wages. The magnifying of economic ends has given wages a primary place in management-labor negotiations, and wages have now become a matter of joint agreement. The amount of the wage, the time of payment, the kind of money to be paid, the basis of payment (hourly, daily, weekly, or by piecework) are now all matters of joint determination. So too are overtime payments for extra hours, for Sundays, and for holidays. The same can be said for the definition of changes in wage rates, in differential payments for skilled and unskilled labor, and for apprentices. In fact, the money expended for labor and the conditions of its distribution have all become matters of joint determination.

Similarly, the hours worked, part-time labor, work distribution in time of slack, the work load, the definition of a "full day's work," job specifications, movement between one job and another, seniority rights in the industry, and many other items that relate to the workers' productive effort are all part of mutual agreement and consent. The joint decisions between labor and management have reached beyond these to the influencing of the size of the labor force, to the conditions of hiring, and to the definition of who may or may not be hired, discharged, laid off, or promoted. It has become a rule and a custom, written into the agreement, to make disciplinary action by the management subject to prescribed rules and procedures. This is also the case in determining the number of shifts to be worked, the speed on automatic operations, the control of safety devices, and the arrangements for health provisions. All of these, as a matter of course, have now come to be joint decisions. The expanding interest of the union has forced management to accept many other items and write them into the basic agreements governing labor relations. Union maintenance, the check-off, the closed shop, the preferential shop, the union hiring hall, the shop steward, the grievance committee, and the arbitration machinery are now part of an accepted pattern. More recently, the labor contract provides for vacations with pay, old-age pensions, displacement wages, sickness insurances, accident insurance, and many other things as well. In fact, this all adds up to a definition of the worker's "right" to his job, and of the union's right to join with management in determining the conditions under which that right is to be exercised.

The collective labor agreement has gone further. In many instances it has attempted to regulate the introduction of new machinery, to control the location of plants, to determine what work can be sent out of the shop, and to lay down the conditions under which an employer may use a subcontractor. It has limited the material an employer may use, and under certain conditions it has influenced pricing policy and distribution. There are now indications that the financial policies, profits, size of the dividend, amortization rate, administrative staff (foremen), personnel policies, and other items may become matters of joint agreement. In fact, we are on the road toward an increasing participation by labor unions in what was hitherto the sole function of management. That management will resist further expansion of union participation is both natural and logical. The definition of its role as that of responsibility for the profitable use of the property entrusted to its care makes it inevitable. But the growing need for stability and security, and the insistence upon motives of "status"—that is, of being a responsible participant in the determination of the conditions under which men spend their lives—make any limitation of trade-union participation temporary, and subject to change with time, experience, precedent, and power. The boundary between management and labor is fluid, and it shifts as each new gain becomes a precedent and a reason for the next step.

The growth of labor responsibility in management is inevitable under contemporary industrial conditions because the trade-union represents all of the life interests of its members. It is, in fact, a "society" with powers of "governance." Management's definition of its own role as that limited by the satisfaction of profit motives places it at a moral and psychological disadvantage and puts it on the defensive.

The major error of the last century has been the assumption that a total society can be organized upon an economic motive, upon profit. The trade-union has proved that notion to be false. It has demonstrated once again that men do not live by bread alone. Because the corporation can offer only bread or cake, it has proved incompetent to meet the demands for the good life. The union, with all its faults, may yet save the corporation and its great efficiencies by incorporating it into its own natural "society," its own cohesive labor force, and by endowing it with the meanings that all real societies possess, meanings that give some substance of idealism to man in his journey between the cradle and the grave. Those meanings cannot be embraced by expanding the economic motive. If the corporation is to survive, it will have to be endowed with a moral role in the world, not merely an economic one. From this point of view, the challenge to management by the trade-union is salutary and hopeful. It is a route, perhaps the only available one, for saving the values of our democratic society, and the contemporary industrial system as well. In some way the corporation and its labor force must become one corporate group and cease to be a house divided and seemingly at war.

If this analysis has any meaning, the trade-union is the conservative force of our time. It is conservative because through bickering over details and by continuous compromise it seeks to preserve the older values by integrating a nonmoral, and therefore essentially corrosive, power (the corporation) into a "society" possessed of an ethical basis for survival. This forced conversion of an institution devoted to the increase of profit as an end is a more promising route for a change-over by the corporation to the values essential to any "society" than is likely to be found through the recently proclaimed doctrines of public responsibility and public service now being avowed in professional management associations.

Not only do the unions share in many of the functions previously enjoyed by management alone, but they also affect the rights of the worker as a citizen in a democratic society. The union stands between the worker and his job. A third party has come into being and has often proved to be stronger than the factory that provides the job opportunity, or the worker who wishes to accept the employment offered. The union is a new "society" in which membership has become essential and in many instances inevitable. This new society has a logic and needs of its own, independent of any given worker or any given job, and it lays down conditions and establishes disciplines for both. The worker cannot get any kind of job he wants. He cannot even learn any trade he wants to, because apprenticeship may be limited, the books of the union may be closed, the initiation fees may be high, or the union may discriminate against him by forcing him to pay for a permit to work without offering an opportunity to become a permanent member of the union. His career in the job he does get is circumscribed by the seniority rules. The amount he can earn is defined for him, his freedom of movement is circumscribed by the fact that he may not be able to enter another industry, or get the same kind of job in another place, and by the fact that if he leaves he may lose his seniority and his rights to promotion and higher wages. If he leaves his union, he will lose his job. He must carry out its policies even if he objects to them. His freedom of criticism and of speech is restricted by the fact that local leaders are in a position to do him injury in ways he cannot escape, or for which he cannot find redress because recognition of these grievances has not as yet become part of either the written or the common law, except in his own organization, and sometimes not even there. He has little influence over the policies of his national union, and that usually only through his own local.

The rights of the worker within his own union are fluid and ill-defined. The constitution of the union may have no definition of forbidden acts, or the local may have a list of its own in addition to those contained in the constitution itself. Where the constitution does enumerate a list of acts that may be punished by the union, they are so vaguely worded as to make it possible for the officers of the union to abuse their powers if they are so minded. Unions can punish their members for such general offenses as disobeying or slandering the union officers, circulating written material without permission of the officers, creating dissension, undermining the union, participating in an outside meeting for a discussion of union business, performing dishonorable acts injurious to the labor movement, strikebreaking, joining another union, working with non-union men, breaking the union's wage policy.[2] The worker tried on these vague charges has a right of appeal from the local, or from the executive board, to the convention of the union, but he may be deprived of his job during the suspension, and the termination of the appeal may take months and years.

The union's constitutional requirements for elections of local officers may be inadequate, and the locally elected officials may, as in the American Federation of Musicians, be removable by the president of the national organization. Conventions for the election of general officers may be rare, as in the International Hod Carriers, Building and Common Laborers Union of America, which held only two conventions in forty-five years.[3] Or the election of the general officers may be influenced by the president's control of the union. In the United Mine Workers the president names the district officers in twenty out of the thirty districts in the union.[4] In the American Federation of Musicians a unit voting system makes it possible for a

[2] P. Taft: "Judicial Procedure in Labor Unions," *Quarterly Journal of Economics*, Vol. LIX, p. 370.

[3] *Hearings*, *I*, p. 1462, "Statement of Vincent F. Morreale, General Counsel, International Hod Carriers, Building and Common Laborers Union of America."

[4] *Hearings*, *V*, p. 1997, "Statement of John L. Lewis, President, United Mine Workers of America."

group of small locals to outvote the large membership in the great cities. In some cases the president's control of the convention machinery may make it possible for him to seat delegates not elected by the local. The convention may have a credentials committee appointed by the president, which seats only "properly accredited delegates," and in a dispute those seated are likely to be acceptable to the president, who may have paid their traveling expenses to the city where the convention is held. The sergeant-at-arms can always dispose of the "improperly accredited" delegate. These grievances may be unusual in the mass, but they are not rare.

The expenses of the administration may be audited by the delegates to the convention; that is, by a committee appointed by the president from the members who are beholden to him and are part of his machine. The officers of the union, as is evidenced by repeated court proceedings, in certain instances have used their power for personal aggrandizement at the expense of the employers, and sometimes at the expense of the workers who are members of the union. The organization exercises police powers in certain jurisdictional strikes, and hires or "entertains," as was recently testified in court, "two thousand men" to keep the "wrong men" from entering the job. Violence, though a decreasing feature of labor controversies, is still not unknown either in strikes or in jurisdictional disputes.

In addition, the worker is taxed by the union not only an initiation fee for admission into it, but monthly or weekly dues, which he must pay, with or without his consent. These grievances have raised the question of the worker's rights within his own organization, as well as the demand for equal opportunity to enter a union if that is the only available means of securing employment. Over three hundred cases of seeming infringement of civil rights have been taken to the courts by union members against their organization. This is an indication of the power of a labor union to interfere with a member's right to bid for a job, or with his right of free speech, or with his right to an accounting of how his money has been spent by the union officials. These questions are bound to become more insistent as the unions become more embracing. A whole body of new law and tradition will have to be developed.

These grievances are merely one side of a question that the trade-unions have to meet. They have to possess sufficient power to discipline their members, or groups of members, who would abuse or pervert their rights and endanger the life of the union itself.

The union must be able to control its members if it is to fulfill the collective agreement, which imposes obligations upon the organization. Wildcat strikes, dissidence fostered for internal political reasons, or attempts to capture the union for ulterior party-line purposes must all be dealt with and controlled. If the union is going to behave as a responsible institution, it needs power to penalize and to expel from its membership those whom it cannot control. But expulsion involves, in certain industries, the power to deny men the means of earning a living, and the abuse of these powers raises questions of civil and constitutional rights of the greatest importance. A union now has powers of "governance" over the lives of its members, and its ability to inflict punishment is very great indeed. Yet it has no adequate common or written law to order the relations between the individual member and the union, or between the local and the national organization. The courts have not wished to interfere in the affairs of a private association and have limited their cognizance to those areas where the member was denied orderly procedure and adjudication as determined by the constitution of the union itself. The worker is presumed to accept the conditions of membership laid down in the constitution and bylaws and to be governed by them. Only when the unions can be shown to have violated their own constitutions have the courts been willing to interfere.

It is doubtful that the ordinary court procedure is the best available instrument for the purpose. In so far as expulsion also involves the loss of employment, the "industrial jurisprudence" embodied in the collective agreement could be expanded to include discipline by and expulsion from the union. The employer or the worker could take a case directly to the existing internal judicial machinery. Such a procedure is already in effect in the agreement between the Boston Consolidated Gas Company and District 50 of the United Mine Workers of America; it provides a board of three for dealing with expulsion, suspension, and exclusion. It will probably be necessary to give these new "judicial boards" powers of enforcement in certain cases and open the way to appeal to the regular courts from their decisions.

The new experiences, reflecting the labor-management complex, call for a new "judiciary," aware of the special questions that need to be dealt with, but free from the costly and time-consuming practices of the ordinary courts. If the right of appeal to the regular courts is retained, and the cost assumed, not by the individual who cannot afford it, but by the joint judicial machinery of labor and management whenever it appears that a real constitutional problem is involved, then it might be easier to protect the worker against his own organization and yet save the union's power to fulfill its great responsibilities.

The growing power of the trade-union must not destroy its democratic tradition. In its origin it is essentially a small democracy. It is based upon equality of members among themselves and implies equal responsibility and opportunity. Its offices are filled by public election, decisions are subject to approval by the members, elections are regular, meetings frequent, debate open and free. The larger the union, the more difficult it becomes to preserve these early democratic practices. But the trade-union will undermine its own existence if it merely becomes a device for bargaining with management. The fealty of its membership, in the long run, will depend upon the union's providing in industry the conditions that will protect the worker's dignity as a man governed by a rule of law, and conserving within the union itself the democratic tradition upon which it rests.

CHAPTER XI

Security and Ownership

THE TRADE-UNION is an attempt by the individual worker to escape from insecurity. In its turn, the trade-union movement has reduced the range of competition in our society. Every activity of organized labor is a denial of both the philosophy and the practice of a free market economy. We have here an unconscious reassertion that man must in some degree be identified with his work, must be attached to it, and must have an attachment for it. Every discussion of shop rules, of efficiency, of grievances, of rights and duties, of obligations and expectancies, embodies the recognition that the relationship between man and his work cannot be defined as purely impersonal, pecuniary, and fluid. The union embraces a concern about the industry, and the feeling, so evident in a thousand past instances, of "this is my job" is but a pathetic restatement that the work and the man belong to each other.

The dramatic character of strikes, boycotts, mass picketing, and public riots has obscured the continuing co-operation between organized labor and mangement, and the role of trade-unions in creating a sense of identity with industry. Even if the union's activity has been restrictive, it has been so on the assumption that the industry is of concern to the union and the workers. One could cite various attempts to specify responsibility and to set up systems of co-operation between labor and management, but these are merely straws in the wind. They are less important because they are often overadvertised and deliberate. More important is the evidence unconsciously revealed when the union insists upon behaving as if it had a permanent stake in the industry. Even the quarrels over the division of the income are indicative. The workers and the owners quarrel over something that seems to belong to both of them. Strikes are from this point of view a healthy and morally promising sign. If the workers are going to quarrel over the division of the product, then they must eventually become concerned with production. The contention over industry's competence to increase wages and the percentage of the wage raise that labor is justified in asking is an indication that unionization involves a commitment to maintain the industry. The attempt to persuade the general public of the justice of their demands by laying before it laborious studies that purport to show that the industries are in fact able to pay the wages asked is further evidence of the same inner compulsion. It is a way of easing a bad conscience, or of establishing a moral right to a larger income from an industry that, it is presumed, even if not asserted, "belongs" to the workers as well as to the owners.

This is merely another way of saying "this is *my* job." It is a different way of asserting an unwitting identity with the source of one's livelihood. The claim that wages can be raised without raising prices, even if made for propaganda purposes only, is of the same order. It recognizes a relationship between wages and prices, and therefore between wages and the cost of production, and, finally, a concern with production itself and the efficiencies that surround it. Recent evidence of this sense of the industry and the union being interdependent is found in the demands for an annual wage and for social benefits to be drawn from production. It is clear that an annual wage can be derived only from a stable and profitable enterprise and can be had only if the workers take their share of responsibility for keeping the enterprise both stable and profitable. They must share with management some of the burdens of reducing costs, improving quality, and increasing production. The raising of the question implies these other commitments even if they are not stated. It would soon become evident that an annual wage, even in the most favorably situated industry, could be had only if there was some agreement on the relationship between costs, prices, productivity, and the annual wage. Otherwise the effort would end in failure or bankruptcy.

This applies to the demands for social security also. If the industry is to become the source of permanent social security, then another attitude, and one inherent in the drive that created trade-unions in the first place, will come into being. The unions, in their own way, though never adequately, have attempted to meet these needs from their own income. Some fifty years ago about thirty American unions already had their own welfare funds. In 1947 eight unions paid out $33,773,023 in benefits from funds derived from their members. This does not include the welfare and security funds supported by employer payments under collective agreements. The International Typographical Union alone paid out $11,483,958 in 1947. In 1949 approximately 3,500,000 workers were beneficiaries of welfare and retirement funds financed by employers and administered by the unions. That was before the spread of the security plans that followed the steel strike in the fall of 1949. The most important social-security activities dependent upon employer financing are those carried on by the International Ladies Garment Workers Union, the Amalgamated Clothing Workers of America, and the United Mine Workers.[1] The initial plans of the International Ladies Garment Workers Union go back to 1942, and in 1948 the Amalgamated Clothing Workers reported that it had a reserve of $50,000,000 in its social-security funds. In 1949 the United Mine Workers paid out $106,840,139 in benefits to 244,168 soft-coal miners and their families.

This suggests the importance of the social-security movement, based upon either union or employer con-

[1] "Union Welfare Funds, Old and New," *Labor and Nation*, September–October 1949, Vol. V, No. 5, p. 105.

tributions. It does not include numerous other forms of industry-supported insurance provisions for the workers. The Standard Oil Company of California spent $54,-000,000 on pension plans in the ten years between 1937 and 1947.[2] In addition, there are many plans for pensions and welfare to which both labor and management contribute. Of the 30 largest oil companies, for instance, 28 have formal pension plans, and 23 of these are based upon contributions by both employers and workers.[3]

Social-security prospects received an important stimulus from the report of the President's Fact-Finding Board in the steel industry. This enunciated a far-reaching, semiofficial doctrine that industry ought to be responsible for the total well-being of all of its employees. While the idea is not new, it has remained for most workers a distant ideal, obtainable gradually if at all, and only over many years. Here, however, we have a Presidential board giving formal approval to the idea and making it the immediate aim of organized labor.

While the principle of social security in industry has worked its way in different degrees into a few industries, it has often been on a worker-industry contributory basis, though there are conspicuous instances where the employers are the sole contributors. These are private arrangements under special conditions, but the Fact-Finding Board proposed a system of social security paid for by the industry, and to be achieved with the blessing, even

[2] *Hearings, II*, p. 452, "Statement of T. S. Petersen, President, Standard Oil Co. of California."

[3] Ibid., p. 451.

if not the active support, of the government. Somewhat modified as a result of the settlements that followed the strikes in the steel industry during the fall of 1949, this proposal has now been adopted by the automobile, rubber, telephone, and other industries. If it becomes general, it will speed a modification in the substance of our industrial relations and will hasten an important change in our economic system.

In theory, labor has been mobile. The contract on both sides was terminable at will. Across the years the trade-union movement has modified this assumed mobility in various ways, but in principle the mobility of labor has not been challenged because no one in a responsible position has questioned the idea of freedom. The proposal set forth by the Presidential Steel Board in effect amounts to the abandonment of the principle of mobility although that was not the intent of the Board. Probably it did not even occur to its members that, if generally accepted, this would be the outcome of the policy they were advocating.

The mobility of labor has been possible because the worker had no investment in the industry in which he worked. Having no investment, he had no responsibility to it. He could leave his job at any moment if a better job were offered to him and be the gainer thereby. He was free because he was irresponsible, and he was irresponsible because he had a day-to-day or hour-to-hour contract, terminable at will. Theoretically, at least, he lost nothing by leaving his job. The principle now introduced, if widely applied, as seems probable, will greatly modify this relationship between the worker and his job. The industry will now assume responsibility for providing his family with medical care, maternity insurance, sickness, old-age and retirement pensions, vacations with pay, and innumerable other services. His current wage will be only a part of his total income, and a decreasing part as his years of service lengthen and as the services expand.

What this really means is that the worker is changing a contract terminable at will to a contract terminable only at death. The worker can, of course, always resign. But where will he go if he does resign? Any other job that he may get will in the vast majority of instances be less advantageous. Union seniority rules will hamper his admission to any other factory or job at his presently held advantage. The principle of cumulative benefits in insurance, vacations, retirement payments, and old-age benefits will work in the same direction. If he goes from one industry to another he will stand to lose his accumulated priorities and privileges. If he goes from one factory to another even in the same industry, or even in the same corporation (as from one Ford factory to another), the seniority rules still apply, and he will lose material advantages sufficiently important to prove a real impediment to the free movement of labor. What is involved in this doctrine is the unconscious substitution of a life contract for a temporary contract. True enough, there is nothing new in the idea. It is the public and official acceptance of it that is new and far-reaching. The essence of the idea was implicit in John L. Lewis's first demand for five cents' royalty on every ton of coal, even if that was the last thing that he thought of when enunciating the new doctrine.

The change implies a good deal more than the immobilization of labor. It implies an identification of the worker's lifelong interests with the fortunes of the industry in which his lot happens to be cast. The future of the steelworkers will now be formally and irretrievably identified with the prosperity of the steel industry, and the same is true of textile workers, automobile workers, and others. Custom and rule will add to the difficulties of leaving. If their social security—their life savings for ill health, vacations, retirement, old age, and death benefits—is to come to them from accumulated rights within the industry, then their commitment to the welfare of the industry becomes a major concern. That is a revolutionary principle in contemporary industrial relations.

The workers must now become psychologically involved in the source of their own livelihood and of their wives' and children's future well-being, for unless the industry is prosperous it will not be able to meet the demands made upon it for today, to say nothing of the future. The implementation of this doctrine will greatly affect the role of the trade-union. It will have to cease being an instrument of war and co-operate with industry to reduce costs and increase production, because only by decreased costs and increased production can growing security demands be met.

This view of the matter raises a whole series of new questions. As long as security has the aspect of a gift, a conquest acquired by a threat of war, or something secured by pressure, it will fail to provide a basis for co-operation, concern, and psychological involvement. It will therefore remain a precarious and temporary acquisition. The future well-being of a million men in the steel industry and their families cannot be built on the threat of war, and war is inevitable as long as the union and the industry consider themselves two separate and antagonistic entities. That concept belies the hope of security for the future and makes it impossible. The workers and their union can find their social security only by becoming integrated with, and within, the industry, as by implication they insist upon being when they cast their whole lives and not merely their jobs upon the fortunes of the steel industry. To achieve these ends they will have to abandon the sense of being a separate and antagonistic power within the industry, assuming no responsibility for its well-being, but demanding increasing benefits at ever higher costs.

These considerations raise the question of the manner in which social security is to be financed. The insistence that it be paid for by the industry itself was a grave error on the part of the President's Board, and a graver one on the part of the leaders of the union. The management of the industry, if it aimed at remaining completely free from trade-union participation in management, if it really wished to keep the industry and the union as two separate and antagonistic elements, ought to have welcomed the proposal that social security should be paid for by the industry itself. It would remain a gift made under duress and withdrawable when necessity or favoring conditions made it possible. The payments would be merely an additional cost to be thrown upon the consumer, saved by internal improvements, or garnered from a reduction of the federal tax. Such a system would represent no structural change in the relationship of the industry to the union or its workers, and presumably it would involve no greater responsibility for the industry on the part of the workers, or concern for their welfare on the part of the industry.

This is not desirable from the point of view of the workers. Their objective, if they throw their security for the future into the hands of the industry, should be to see to it that the industry is competent to meet their needs. Otherwise the demand itself makes no sense. They cannot bankrupt the industry in the pursuit of their own security. Joint contribution would make for joint ownership and management of their investment. It would make for a realistic joint study of the future needs of the industry, and increasing co-operation.

There is another principle to be considered. Security and wages are not synonymous and in any given instance may be antagonistic. This raises the question of the relationship between a daily wage and real income. Real income can be measured only in terms of a lifetime, for it involves the well-being of an entire family, a whole generation. A wage, on the other hand, may be hourly, daily, or weekly, and its bearing on social security may or may not be favorable. From the worker's point of view, security has been, and remains, the major interest. From the employer's point of view, the easiest relationship is a contractual wage, terminable at will. The whole life is involved in the first instance, a temporary obligation in the latter. If the present movement for social security is not to be diverted to a new form of the older wage dispute, then trade-union leadership must make it a vehicle for increasing responsibility by the trade-unions within industry. The condition of status for the individual which the trade-union movement has been fostering by every rule it has written into the collective agreements can be achieved only in an industrial structure in which the lifelong interests of the workers are commensurate with their responsibilities. This means that the union must acquire expanding rights of ownership in the industry. And such a step is an inevitable by-product of the demand for lifelong security.

The accumulation of social-security funds will ultimately involve their investment, in part at least in the industry from which they are drawn. The process has already begun, although it will be long in maturing. It took over a century for a free market to dominate the economy to such a degree that it pulled a large part of the energies of men in the Western World into its orbit, though even here it never completely embraced all of the economic activities of the modern world. It may take just as long for the newer movement to achieve a similar impact upon the mass of men. But the older division between labor and industry is breaking down, and the growth of a lifelong integration between the worker and his job is visible, even if it takes generations to complete, even if it never fully embraces all men laboring for a living.

This change, hidden in the present development, has another basis of institutional logic. Under the name of dues the trade-unions have re-established the older head-tax for their own members. These are collected as a matter of course under the provisions of collective agreements, and during the war under sanction of the government. As a result, the unions have become repositories of large and continuously growing funds. They have, like the insurance companies, become semipublic savings institutions. The annual income of United States trade-unions is estimated at one billion dollars, half of which is set aside for some form of social security. The assets of the local and national unions are placed at a minimum of three billion dollars.[4] Many unions have an annual income from dues alone of over a million dollars.

In 1947 the International Ladies Garment Workers Union received $3,500,000 from dues. The Amalgamated Clothing Workers received $3,300,000 in 1946; the Textile Workers of America, $3,600,000; the United States Steel Workers, $3,900,000. The Brotherhood of Painters, Decorators and Paperhangers of America had an income of $8,374,453 between July 1, 1941 and June 30, 1946. A relatively small union, the Packinghouse Workers of America, has an annual income of over $800,000.

When the union's relations with management are

[4] Alexander Lipset: *Labor's Partnership in Industrial Enterprises* (New York: Floyd L. Carlisle, Inc.; 1950).

stabilized, the expenditures for strikes and strike benefits are a fraction of its income. For instance, the International Ladies Garment Workers Union spent $56,376, and the Amalgamated Clothing Workers $45,131, while income from dues alone was over $3,000,000.

These funds from dues are a fraction of what the income from social-security benefits promises to be. We have already seen that the Amalgamated Clothing Workers have a fifty-million-dollar reserve insurance fund, and the income from the mines has been placed at over $132,000,000 a year for the miners. It has been estimated that employers are now paying one billion dollars for labor pension systems alone.[5]

It is only logical that some of these funds should be reinvested in the industry from which they come. Presumably the large sums ultimately involved cannot be withdrawn from industry without seriously affecting the economy, and, furthermore, such investment is dictated by the logic of the union's position. It cannot insist on greater participation in and concern for the industry except upon a proprietary basis. The United Automobile Workers have already bought into sixty-eight companies in which the union has collective agreements. The unions are now investing considerable funds in United States Government bonds, in real estate, in insurance companies of their own, and in other enterprises. These are at best expedients.

A new source of investment from these semipublic agencies is being opened up at a time when a tendency

[5] *Reporter*, May 10, 1949, p. 161.

to equalize incomes and reduce the great fortunes makes it less likely that large private savings will continue to be available. Thus one of the changes hidden in the growth of trade-unionism is the re-establishment of a proprietary interest by the workers in the industries from which they draw their living. For the worker, at least, the day of fluidity, impersonality and irresponsibility is drawing to a close. If he is going to have a pecuniary interest, he will also have to assume the moral responsibilities that a pecuniary relationship has always involved: responsibility for the property he owns, the work he does, and the quality of what he produces for the rest of the community.

There is nothing in law, morals, or public policy that is contrary to the growth of proprietary interest by the workers through their organizations, as a result of the cumulative savings that are now accruing to them on an ever increasing scale. It is not likely that these new savings institutions, for so the unions may be considered, will ever own all of modern industry. That is not necessary, and perhaps not even possible. But increasing ownership is a logical next step, and with it increasing responsibility. These developments require a reorganization of the educational system to make possible the intellectual and creative identity of the men at work with the industry in which they work. A new system of industrial education, already envisaged in many incipient efforts both in industry and in trade-unions, is bound to be part of the process so that men may see and understand their own place in the large and technical industries in which they are immersed, as well as industry's place in the scheme of the economy as a whole.

What is presumed in this development is that the union will gradually take on the role of the modern corporation by buying into it, and that ownership will cease to be fluid and impersonal. This change-over will raise as many difficulties as it will eliminate. It will re-establish a society of status, the "estates" of an older day, with all of the restrictions upon personal mobility and personal freedom. But, in a measure, it has already done that. It will raise deep issues of civil rights, and will trouble the relationship of a democratic government to these new, powerful, semipublic corporations.

These difficulties already exist: the corporation versus the state, the cartel versus the state, the national union versus the state. The relationships of these bodies to each other and to the government will, of necessity, become the major source of both common and written law, and of public policy. The dealings between the union, proprietary corporation, and management will continue to be a matter of grave concern. And the management will be plagued by questions of efficiency, technical change, free decision, corruption, pull, pressure, and interference. There is no reason, however, to assume these difficulties are insurmountable, or that they will create graver conflicts than those the industrial system has weathered in the last hundred and fifty years. Presumably the growth of proprietary ownership on the part of the unions will be slow. Their share of the directorships will long remain a minority if fortune is on their side long enough for these new owners to acquire the necessary insight and restraint to accommodate themselves to the complexities and exactions of modern management. It will prove something of a trial, but perhaps not an unwelcome one, for management to find itself accountable to a corporation where ownership and responsibility are united rather than divorced.

These are the visible trends in our society. This is the seeming outcome of the drift of our time. The present economy cannot rest for long on a system of fluid, impersonal ownership and fluid, impersonal labor. Labor, in many instances, has already ceased to be either fluid or impersonal. If the presently implicit outcome is not in the cards, what are the alternatives to what is a non-enduring structure? The obvious answer is state ownership, socialism, communism, state capitalism, expropriation, confiscation, revolution, or what not. But state ownership and control, the essence of which is the same regardless of the name, are essentially a political solution. By its nature a political solution is unstable and temporary. Industrial activity is conditioned by disciplines that tend to be automatic and impersonal. He who neglects his business loses it or goes bankrupt; he who neglects his job finds himself out of work. Even a trade-union cannot impose upon an industry restrictions that destroy its powers of survival without also committing suicide. These automatic sanctions are neither perfect nor always timely, but on the whole they have proved sufficiently effective to make possible a growing and increasingly complex industrial system. Both management and labor have, with many failures in between, fulfilled their necessary roles without any imputation that the failure of a business or the loss of a job was due to criminal intent requiring legal sanctions.

When the state operates the industry, every failure, every negligence, every bit of soldiering on the job, every strike, every criticism, every demand for a change, even the failure to come to work, or unavoidable accident, may be taken as opposition to the state. Economic sanctions cease to be directly operative because political prestige requires that failure be hidden, excused, or converted into a charge of deliberate negligence or conspiracy. What was impersonal discipline becomes converted into sanctions imposed by administrative boards or judicial bodies. What was a strike becomes a rebellion, and what was an accident becomes sabotage. When an industry is nationalized, a strike is against the government, and strikes become politically suspect. Historically sanctioned and habitual behavior is redefined in hostile political terms. This applies not merely to strikes, but to all industrial frictions. The absentee, the late-comer, the inefficient worker, the trouble-maker, he who is involved in an accident or an industrial mishap, becomes suspect and subject to political sanctions. The only discipline the state can fall back upon is the police power.

It is predictable that every state, including Great Britain, must end as a police state if the government becomes the arbiter of the innumerable incidents and accidents of industrial life. The bitterness of trade-union leaders in Great Britain against workers who disobey the government rules, or the trade-union rules, suggests the trend of government policy. The readiness to use soldiers to displace workers in a strike, and the demand even by trade-union leaders in the government for greater control over labor mobility, are the adumbrations of what will, in time, if the situation continues, become a police state in the name of freedom. The ordinary relations between men for which nonpolitical sanctions have always been operative are being redefined in political terms for which only political sanctions are in the end available.

Serious as are these considerations, there are others of even greater weight in the transfer of management from private to governmental auspices. It has long been a truism in politics that he who may not utter a wrong opinion is not free to utter a correct one. One who has not the freedom to be wrong cannot have the freedom to be right. If that is true in politics, it is infinitely more so in economic life. The number of mistakes in judgment men make in business is great indeed. These errors must be somewhat less than the accurate forecasts, because the industrial system has both survived and provided an increasing material income for the mass of the people. If an industry is to survive, it must make some good judgments, or bankruptcy will inevitably overtake it. Even the most successful enterprise, however, has a record of poor investments, poor management, unforeseen obstacles, and biased optimism. It succeeded because it was more frequently right than wrong. But unless it was free to be wrong, it could not have made any judgments at all.

In some measure the industrial system has been built upon the mistakes and failures that have strewn its path because men were free to make the mistakes. Freedom to evaluate the various forces at play, even at the risk of economic failure, is the only basis upon which any complex industry or industrial system can survive. It is obvious from our available experience that such freedom cannot exist in a society where the state controls the industrial system.

Political considerations and their punitive implications put a political premium on right guesses; therefore, a political penalty on wrong ones, which means, in effect, that no one feels free to make any judgment whatsoever. Only those at the very top, because they can temporarily at least hide their poor estimates and failures by falling back upon the public treasury, or upon the cry of political sabotage, can feel free to make a decision. What is involved is a change from the flexible, many-sided, and frequently contradictory play of many minds and purposes, where numerous judgments are made by large numbers involved in the same process, the errors checking one another because most of the decisions affect only fractions of the total enterprise, to one where nobody feels free to make any decision because of its possible political implications. The responsibility is therefore shifted from shoulder to shoulder until the final judgment comes from the one source that seems politically immune. The gravity of an error made at that level cannot be checked out by other decisions, because there are no others, and the consequences are hidden if possible, or diverted politically, even in good faith, by putting the blame for the failure on the "enemy," hidden or open. It is clear that no complex industrial society can continue yielding a growing income for the mass of the people under such conditions, or even survive as a going concern.

Of equal importance, however, is the need for a free flow of inventiveness within the system. If industrial society has expanded over the last hundred and fifty years, it has been because there existed a peculiar moral and psychological milieu that stimulated and brought into being these almost infinitely variable ideas and processes and provided a testing-ground for them. Here, too, of course, there are numerous instances of failure, insufficient use, misuse, or even deliberate suppression of new inventions. But, on the record, industrial society has absorbed, and is today absorbing, a constant stream of new techniques and processes. Without them it could not have developed the complexities and efficiencies it boasts.

It is probably equally true that the constant flow of new inventions is essential to the survival of the present industrial system even at its present level of activity. If new inventions were to cease flowing into the system, it would gradually deteriorate and its manifold threads unwind. It remains to be proved that these conditions favoring a free flow of ingenuity can be reproduced in any other society. They never have occurred, and there are strong considerations for assuming that they cannot, in a system of imposed uniformities implicit in a centralized economy under governmental control.

To date, Russian industrialization has existed largely by copying the technology, the designs, and the processes of the Western World, especially those of the United States. That, after all, is a comparatively simple undertaking, especially when engineers, technicians, models, and co-operating agencies of various sorts have been made available, from Ford factories to General Electric plants. When it has copied what we had, will the Russian experiment then provide the moral setting for that flow of new inventions needed to keep the system a going and developing concern? That is the crux of the problem, for only upon that basis can it continue to increase its equipment in capital goods and provide an expanding flow of consumer goods to raise the standard of living of its people.

In spite of its many shortcomings, it is not the industrial society of the Western World that is on trial. That has now been tried for over a hundred and fifty years and has given men a greater body of material goods than was ever enjoyed by the mass of men anywhere. What is on trial is the new system that would replace it on grounds of higher efficiency and greater moral perfection. But the conditions that made the technological development and industrial growth of the present economy possible—freedom of judgment and of error, and the milieu for a free flow of inventions, all implying the private ingenuity and concern of innumerable men unimpeded by political consideration—are being denied. Time will ultimately decide this debate, but it is the Russian experiment and the experiment in Great Britain and in other areas that are on trial before the world. They still have to demonstrate that, in terms of an increasing material well-being, personal freedom, the flow of human ingenuity, and the growth of personal dignity, they can do as well as the economy they would displace.

There is another consideration that needs to be pondered. The Russian economy is relatively simple. If Russia is really to become an industrial nation, then it will follow, as it has in Great Britain and the United States, that the vast majority of the people will be drawn into a complex vortex of industrial activities. It will require that higher education be given to large numbers of its people. It will also require that millions of them acquire the freedom of making an infinite variety of decisions demanded by an expanding industry. This means immediate decisions that cannot wait for political consent and that in the nature of the case must be wrong decisions perhaps half of the time.

Without such freedom no modern industrial society can be built, and if the freedom exists, then state controls and police sanctions cannot survive. The Russian system thus has the seeds of its own destruction embedded in it. It aspires to a higher material well-being for the mass of its people. It cannot provide it without becoming a great industrial society and cannot become a great industrial society without freedom of private judgment in infinitely variable instances. If such freedom comes into being, as it must if industry is to develop, then the freedom will destroy the present police state.

The police state can survive only in a comparatively

simple agricultural society. It will meet its destruction at the hands of a growing industrialism. The dilemma is clear. Soviet Russia cannot give up the ideal of an expanding standard of living, and it cannot achieve it without committing suicide.

This discussion of the nature and implications of state ownership as an alternative to the present tendency of trade-unions to become trade-union corporations makes it plain that what is being proposed by Socialists and Communists is not a satisfactory substitute for our present system, nor a satisfactory solution for our present difficulties. It is all too clear that, to maintain its hold, government, simply because any political solution is unstable, will be forced to develop policies that are arbitrary in their nature and are dictated by political considerations.

All of the charges made against the Nazi and Communist management will be made in time against any system of government control. Industrial society is too complex, many-sided, subtle, unstable, changeable, and creative to be handled by political dicta and for political considerations. Government control is unstable because it can operate only through repression. In the end either the organic groups now in unions will destroy the authoritarian government state, or the government will end by stifling the industries and ultimately disintegrating them.

The trade-union is the real alternative to the authoritarian state. The trade-union is our modern "society," the only true society that industrialism has fostered. As a true society it is concerned with the whole man, and embodies the possibilities of both the freedom and the security essential to human dignity. The corporation and the union will ultimately merge in common ownership and cease to be a house divided. It is only thus that a common identity may once again come to rule the lives of men and endow each one with rights and duties recognized by all.

A NOTE ON THE TYPE

This book is set on the Linotype in Caslon, a modern adaptation of a type designed by the first William Caslon (1692–1766). The Caslon face has had two centuries of ever increasing popularity in the United States. It is of interest to note that the first copies of the Declaration of Independence and the first paper currency distributed to the citizens of the new-born nation were printed in this type face.

Composed, printed, and bound by *Vail-Ballou Press, Inc.*,
Binghamton, N. Y.